Tabletops, Floors, an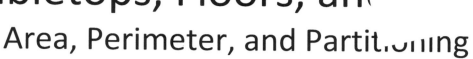
Area, Perimeter, and Partitioning

Sylvia Glassco
Rebecca Kotler
Catherine Twomey Fosnot

New Perspectives on Learning, LLC
1194 Ocean Avenue
New London, CT 06320

ISBN: 0997688610
ISBN-13: 978-0997688610

Table of Contents

Unit Overview

The focus of this unit is twofold: 1) the analysis of shapes by their properties with the understanding of class inclusion—that shapes can be classified in more than one category (for example, a square is also a rectangle and both are quadrilaterals); and 2) the introduction of perimeter and area of rectangles, including the generation of the general formulas.

The unit is based on the results of research by Huang and Witz (2011), which revealed that the geometric operations of superimposition, decomposition, and re-composition, as well as the concept of congruence, are essential precursors for the conceptualization of the formulas for area measurement. The unit is composed of a series of investigations beginning with the context of teachers considering various table arrangements in their classrooms. Students consider how much area each child gets as a workspace if the various tabletops are partitioned equally, four children to a table. Engaging children in the equipartitioning of tabletop surfaces supports the development of conservation of area—the recognition that resulting shapes do not need to be congruent to have equivalent areas. As the unit progresses the area and perimeter of each of two classrooms become the focus and at the end of the unit children investigate the area of the 50 by 30 meter school sports field.

Several minilessons are included in the unit as well; some provide opportunities for children to explore shapes by their properties and to sort and categorize using them. Other minilessons are structured as strings of related multiplication problems explicitly designed to guide learners toward computational fluency with an emphasis on the use of the associative and commutative properties. The open array model is used to represent students' strategies to further develop the area model.

The unit is designed to align with the CCSS Standards of Practice and the following core objectives:

Reason with shapes and their attributes.

- CCSS.Math.Content.3.G.A.1
  Understand that shapes in different categories (e.g., rhombi, rectangles, and others) may share attributes (e.g., having four sides), and that the shared attributes can define a larger category (e.g., quadrilaterals). Recognize rhombi, rectangles, and squares as examples of quadrilaterals, and draw examples of quadrilaterals that do not belong to any of these subcategories.

- CCSS.Math.Content.3.G.A.2
  Partition shapes into parts with equal areas. Express the area of each part as a unit fraction of the whole. *For example, partition a shape into 4 parts with equal area, and describe the area of each part as 1/4 of the area of the shape.*

Geometric measurement: understand concepts of area and relate area to multiplication and to addition.

- CCSS.Math.Content.3.MD.C.5
  Recognize area as an attribute of plane figures and understand concepts of area measurement.

- CCSS.Math.Content.3.MD.C.5.a
  A square with side length 1 unit, called "a unit square," is said to have "one square unit" of area, and can be used to measure area.

- CCSS.Math.Content.3.MD.C.5.b
  A plane figure which can be covered without gaps or overlaps by n unit squares is said to have an area of n square units.

- CCSS.Math.Content.3.MD.C.6
  Measure areas by counting unit squares (square cm, m in, ft, and improvised units).

- CCSS.Math.Content.3.MD.C.7
  Relate area to the operations of multiplication and addition.

- CCSS.Math.Content.3.MD.C.7.a
  Find the area of a rectangle with whole-number side lengths by tiling it, and show that the area is the same as would be found by multiplying the side lengths.

- CCSS.Math.Content.3.MD.C.7.b
  Multiply side lengths to find areas of rectangles with whole-number side lengths in the context of solving real world and mathematical problems, and represent whole-number products as rectangular areas in mathematical reasoning.

- CCSS.Math.Content.3.MD.C.7.c
  Use tiling to show in a concrete case that the area of a rectangle with whole-number side lengths a and $b + c$ is the sum of $a \times b$ and $a \times c$. Use area models to represent the distributive property in mathematical reasoning.

- CCSS.Math.Content.3.MD.C.7.d
  Recognize area as additive. Find areas of rectilinear figures by decomposing them into non-overlapping rectangles and adding the areas of the non-overlapping parts, applying this technique to solve real world problems.

Geometric measurement: recognize perimeter.

- CCSS.Math.Content.3.MD.D.8
  Solve real world and mathematical problems involving perimeters of polygons, including finding the perimeter given the side lengths, finding an unknown side length, and exhibiting rectangles with the same perimeter and different areas or with the same area and different perimeters.

The Landscape of Learning

BIG IDEAS

- ❖ Conservation of length
- ❖ Perimeter is the distance around an enclosed area and is measured with linear units
- ❖ One line can define two bounded areas simultaneously
- ❖ Area can be measured by covering and counting non-overlapping units
- ❖ A square unit of area in a rectangular array is simultaneously in a row and a column
- ❖ A square with side length 1 unit, called "a unit square," is said to have "one square unit" of area, and can be used to measure area.
- ❖ Conservation of area
- ❖ Groups can be regrouped
- ❖ The commutative property of multiplication
- ❖ The distributive property of multiplication
- ❖ The associative property of multiplication
- ❖ 2 x (L + W) of a rectangle equals the perimeter
- ❖ Equipartitioning of area results in equivalent areas even if the resulting shapes are not congruent
- ❖ Shapes can be made with other shapes
- ❖ The linear dimensions of length and width of rectangles can be multiplied to produce a square unit measurement of total area
- ❖ Shapes can have equal perimeters but different areas (or equal areas and different perimeters)

STRATEGIES

- ❖ Covers a space, but overlaps units or leaves gaps
- ❖ Partitions a shape with lines
- ❖ Counts external or internal squares to determine perimeter
- ❖ Counts linear units to determine perimeter
- ❖ Adds the lengths of the sides to determine perimeter
- ❖ Filling and counting
- ❖ Skip counting
- ❖ Repeated addition
- ❖ Partial products
- ❖ Doubling
- ❖ Doubling and halving
- ❖ Factoring and grouping flexibly
- ❖ Partitioning a shape
- ❖ Uses generalizable forms of perimeter formulas
- ❖ Uses generalizable forms of area formulas
- ❖ Uses generalized forms of perimeter and area formulas to find unknowns

MODELS

- ❖ Number Line
- ❖ Grid
- ❖ Open Array

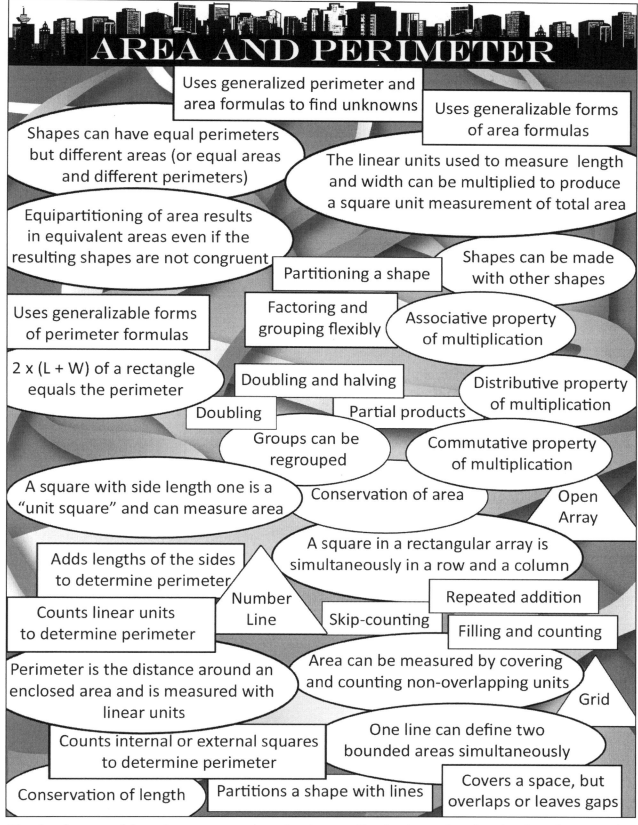

AREA AND PERIMETER

Uses generalized perimeter and area formulas to find unknowns

Uses generalizable forms of area formulas

Shapes can have equal perimeters but different areas (or equal areas and different perimeters)

The linear units used to measure length and width can be multiplied to produce a square unit measurement of total area

Equipartitioning of area results in equivalent areas even if the resulting shapes are not congruent

Partitioning a shape

Shapes can be made with other shapes

Uses generalizable forms of perimeter formulas

Factoring and grouping flexibly

Associative property of multiplication

2 x (L + W) of a rectangle equals the perimeter

Doubling and halving

Distributive property of multiplication

Doubling

Partial products

Groups can be regrouped

Commutative property of multiplication

A square with side length one is a "unit square" and can measure area

Conservation of area

Open Array

Adds lengths of the sides to determine perimeter

A square in a rectangular array is simultaneously in a row and a column

Number Line

Repeated addition

Counts linear units to determine perimeter

Skip-counting

Filling and counting

Perimeter is the distance around an enclosed area and is measured with linear units

Area can be measured by covering and counting non-overlapping units

Grid

Counts internal or external squares to determine perimeter

One line can define two bounded areas simultaneously

Conservation of length

Partitions a shape with lines

Covers a space, but overlaps or leaves gaps

The landscape of learning: area and perimeter on the horizon showing landmark strategies (rectangles), big ideas (ovals), and models (triangles).

The Mathematical Landscape

For area and the partitioning of it, as for multiplication in general, the array model can be a powerful tool. An array can be used to represent partial products, and the relationship of these parts to the total area can help students develop an understanding of the distributive, associative, and commutative properties of multiplication. Research by Battista et al. (1998), however, suggests that the array model is often difficult for learners to understand because the ability to coordinate rows and columns simultaneously requires a substantial cognitive reorganization—and thus an understanding of arrays develops through successive stages. The unit in this series that supports the early development of the array model is *Muffles' Truffles.*

Tabletops, Floors, and Fields: Area, Perimeter, and Partitioning assumes some prior knowledge of linear measurement (for example, see *Farms and Fences*) and of rectangular arrays (for example, see *Muffles' Truffles*), as it is designed to extend the grid model to an area model.

BIG IDEAS

This unit is designed to encourage the development of some of the big ideas related to multiplication and their use with geometry—measuring and calculating perimeter and area of rectangles and studying the relationship between the two measurements.

These big ideas include:
- ❖ *Conservation of length*
- ❖ *Perimeter is the distance around an enclosed area and is measured with linear units*
- ❖ *One line can represent two bounded areas simultaneously*
- ❖ *Area can be measured by covering and counting non-overlapping units*
- ❖ *A square unit of area in a rectangular array is simultaneously in a row and a column*
- ❖ *A square with side length 1 unit, called "a unit square," is said to have "one square unit" of area, and can be used to measure area.*
- ❖ *Conservation of area*
- ❖ *The commutative property of multiplication*
- ❖ *The distributive property of multiplication*
- ❖ *The associative property of multiplication*
- ❖ *2 x (L + W) of a rectangle equals the perimeter*
- ❖ *Equipartitioning of area results in equivalent areas even if the resulting shapes are not congruent*
- ❖ *Shapes can be made with other shapes*
- ❖ *The linear dimensions of length and width of rectangles can be multiplied to produce a square unit measurement of total area*
- ❖ *Shapes can have equal perimeters but different areas (or equal areas and different perimeters)*

❖ *Conservation of length*

Early in the development of an understanding of length measurement, children think that the length of a zigzagged fence may be shorter than the same length when straightened (Piaget, Inhelder, and

Szeminska, 1960). They may argue that a side of a fence on two sides of a rectangular shape (length plus width) is not the same length as when that section of fence is straightened out into one line. They need many opportunities to measure and transform the segments of fencing into one straight line to construct this idea. Eventually an understanding that the length is conserved develops and children are able to explore and defend how lengths can be equivalent even when they are not straight lines, look different, and are comprised of different smaller lengths.

❖ *Perimeter is the distance around an enclosed area and is measured with linear units.*

Children often confuse area and perimeter, primarily because the concepts are taught as formulas and the big ideas related to them are neglected. Perimeter is not as easily understood by children as one might think. Conservation of length is a necessary precursor to the idea that the sum of the lengths of the sides is equivalent to the total distance around the shape.

❖ *One line can represent two bounded areas simultaneously*

Even when children begin to understand that shapes can be decomposed and composed into other shapes, they continue to believe that boundaries cannot be shared. When drawing two adjacent triangles to make a rhombus, they want to draw each line segment of each triangle and thus they produce 2 lines for the diameter. Initially this is because now they have a strong understanding of the Euclidean properties of each shape and thus they think it is necessary to represent them (Goodnow, 1977). The idea that one line can simultaneously represent a border between the two triangles (for example using one line across the diameter of the rhombus to represent two triangular areas) is huge and requires cognitive reorganization—definitely a big idea for our young mathematicians!

❖ *Area can be measured by covering and counting non-overlapping units*

Whereas perimeter involves the measurement of length, area is about covering (and measuring) the enclosed space. For children to understand the difference they need ample opportunities to cover or tile the space inside shapes. At first they may not understand that gaps and overlapping matter. In the investigation on Day One of this unit, you may see some children who draw four separate areas on the tabletop, but leave some of the tabletop space out. They may not yet understand that one line can represent the shared boundary, or they may not yet understand that gaps and overlapping matter when measuring area.

❖ *A square unit of area in a rectangular array is simultaneously in a row and a column.*

Understanding how arrays are made with aligned rows and columns requires children to think about two dimensions simultaneously (Battista et al. 1998). Every square in a row is also in a column. Notice how children count the tiles. Do they realize that each row is a group and that each row has the same number of squares and skip count, or do they count by ones, maybe even across and down, then across the bottom and up the other side? Do they count some squares twice? Coordinating the two dimensions is what will bring students to abandon inefficient counting strategies in favor of repeated addition and/or multiplication. Supporting children to draw lines to make grids versus drawing individual squares may help them begin to consider how each square is in a row and a column simultaneously (Outhred and Mitchelmore, 2004). This big idea is a precursor to understanding how L x W can produce a measurement for area.

❖ *A square with side length 1 unit, called a "unit square," is said to have "one square unit" of area, and can be used to measure area.*

Understanding that the linear units used to measure lengths and widths of rectangles become square units when multiplied can sometimes be tricky for students. If students have explored *Muffles' Truffles* they will likely have already constructed this idea, but you may find some students who still find this relationship elusive.

❖ *Conservation of area*

It is the tiling (or gridding) of various rectangles that eventually helps children construct the idea that shapes do not have to be congruent to have equivalent areas. Early on, children may even think that a non-square rectangle rotated (from a horizontal position to a vertical one) may have gained in area. Decomposition and composition, building arrays, and determining the area of different sizes of rectangles affords children opportunities to consider how pieces of an array can be moved without affecting the overall area.

❖ *The commutative property of multiplication*

Multiplication is commutative: a x b = b x a. Picture a rectangular array (drawn on graph paper), measuring 4 inches by 19 inches. If we turn this array 90 degrees, we have a 19 x 4 array. Using arrays like this is exactly what students do to convince each other of the commutative property. When multiplying, they come to realize that no matter how the array is rotated, the area is the same.

❖ *The distributive property of multiplication*

The distributive property of multiplication is central to the standard multiplication algorithm: a x (b + c) = (a x b) + (a x c). This property can be thought of as splitting a rectangular array (or area) into smaller pieces such that, for example, 6 x 24 becomes 6 x 20 and 6 x 4. Similarly, pieces can be joined to form a single array.

❖ *The associative property of multiplication*

The associative property also holds for multiplication: (a x b) x c = a x (b x c). Factors can be associated flexibly without changing the area. Picture an array measuring 50 by 30. Imagine cutting it into halves, each measuring 50 by 15. The pieces can now be rearranged to form a new rectangle measuring 100 by 15. The dimensions may have changed but the area did not: (50x2) x 15 = 50 x (2x15). As students work towards fluent multiplication, and its use in calculating area, they will find this property very helpful.

❖ 2 x (L + W) of a rectangle equals the perimeter

As children come to understand that the sum of the side lengths is equal to the total perimeter, they most often proceed by adding all four lengths. The insight that the length and width can be doubled is early multiplicative structuring (in contrast to additive structuring) and is a major turning point in development. 2L + 2W = 2(L+W) is actually a specific case of the distributive property and requires that children be able to see L + W as a new unit of length and half of the total perimeter.

❖ Equipartitioning of area results in equivalent areas even if the resulting shapes are not congruent

To cut a rectangle into four equivalent sections using bisecting lines requires an understanding that one line can represent two bounded areas simultaneously and, in the case of diagonal lines, to also understand that shapes do not have to be congruent to have equivalent areas. The investigations in the first few days of this unit provide children with opportunities to explore and construct these ideas. One child may partition a rectangle into four equal triangular shapes, while another produces four smaller rectangles, but each section is ¼ of the whole. Be prepared to facilitate rich conversations and proofs on whether these shapes that look quite different have equivalent areas.

❖ Shapes can be made with other shapes

Realizing that different shapes can enclose equivalent areas is a huge developmental leap for children. This idea requires an integration and synthesis of part/whole relations. It is in fact an important precursor to developing the ideas of composing and decomposing areas, which will be needed much later in development (in other grades) as they engage in constructing area formulas for polygons.

❖ The linear dimensions of length and width of rectangles can be multiplied to produce a square unit measurement of total area

The shift from additive structuring (counting or adding squares) to multiplicative structuring (LxW=A) is a big one. Not only do children have to understand the relationship of rows and columns, they have to construct the idea that the number of squares in each row is the same, and that the number of tiles in the columns can be used to designate the number of rows (and therefore the number of groups). Further, the linear unit used in measuring length and width is the sum of the lengths of the edge of each square. So much cognitive reordering is involved in the construction of area!

❖ Shapes can have equal perimeters but different areas (or equal areas and different perimeters)

At first children may think that shapes with equivalent areas must also have equivalent perimeters (and that shapes with equal perimeters must have equivalent areas). As they explore the areas of various classrooms in the second investigation in this unit, students are usually quite surprised to find that two rooms with equal perimeters in fact have different areas. In later grades they will examine the relationship of area and perimeter in more depth and eventually come to understand that as the dimensions of a given perimeter of a polygon approach equivalence, the area increases. In this unit children are not expected to reach this general conclusion, but the examination of the relationship is the beginning of the journey!

STRATEGIES

As you work with the activities in this unit, you will notice that students will use many strategies to solve the problems that are posed to them. Here are some strategies to notice:

❖ *Covers a space, but overlaps units or leaves gaps*
❖ *Partitions a shape with lines*
❖ *Counts external or internal squares to determine perimeter*
❖ *Counts linear units to determine perimeter*
❖ *Adds the lengths of the sides to determine perimeter*
❖ *Filling and counting*
❖ *Skip-counting*
❖ *Repeated addition*
❖ *Partial products*
❖ *Doubling*
❖ *Doubling and halving*
❖ *Partitioning a shape*
❖ *Factoring and grouping flexibly*
❖ *Uses generalizable forms of perimeter formulas*
❖ *Uses generalizable forms of area formulas*
❖ *Uses generalizable forms of perimeter and area formulas to find unknowns*

❖ *Covers a space, but overlaps units or leaves gaps*
A child may fill a space with tiles but overlap squares, or leave gaps between them.

❖ *Partitions a shape with lines*
A child draws lines to cut the space into sections rather than drawing individual tiles.

❖ *Counts internal or external squares to determine perimeter*
As students initially begin to grapple with area and perimeter, they often count boxes bordering a line rather than the line segments themselves which can lead to over- or under-counting.

❖ *Counts linear units to determine perimeter*
When children solidly construct that perimeter is composed of linear units, rather than "squares" or "tiles," they often count the units bordering a shape, particularly with irregular shapes, to determine the perimeter.

❖ Adds side lengths to determine perimeter

As students begin to structure line segments in the grid as portions of a length (and conserve length) they come to recognize that opposite sides of a rectangle have the same number of line segments) and they add the side lengths to determine the perimeter.

❖ Filling and Counting

When students do not have a strong understanding of how arrays are composed of rows and columns—that any given square is part of a row and column simultaneously—the only way they can determine area is to fill the space and count the squares by ones. It is important as you work with students such as these that you support them to see how skip counting by rows or columns is more efficient than counting by ones—but be sure they see where the groups are coming from!

❖ Skip-counting

As students count by ones, the struggle to keep track coupled with the development of the idea that arrays are composed of rows and columns, which can be seen as groups, produces skip-counting. Although students who exhibit this strategy are still structuring additively rather than multiplicatively, it is an advance from counting by ones because they are now grouping.

❖ Repeated addition

Repeated addition is another example of structuring the task additively. Precisely because skip-counting can be difficult, you may find students writing down the number in each row, and then adding repeatedly. This adding is also cumbersome, however, and students may regroup the groups to add more efficiently. This regrouping is an important strategy that is a precursor to the emergence of partial products and doubling and halving.

❖ Partial products

An important shift in multiplicative thinking occurs when students regroup the groups and make partial products—they use a fact they know to make another. For example, to compute
6 x 24, they might make use of 6 x 20 and then add 6 more groups of 4.

❖ Doubling

Doubling marks the beginning of multiplicative structuring and scaling. To solve 20 x 6, students might use 10 x 6 and double it. Doubling is also a precursor to the simultaneous use of doubling and halving.

❖ Doubling and halving

Rather than making use of ten times, some students may pair numbers when they regroup groups during addition. For example, when solving 30 x 50 they may make groups of 100. Now, instead of 30 groups of 50, they have 15 groups of 100. Although this strategy emerges out of additive structuring, it is a specific case of the associative property of multiplication: 50 x (2 x 15) = (50 x 2) x 15. The minilessons interspersed throughout the unit are designed to encourage students to develop their understanding of this property and to use it when doing mental arithmetic; to factor and group flexibly when it is helpful.

❖ Partitioning a shape

As students develop an understanding of the distributive property, they may slice a shape into smaller pieces for which they can calculate the area more easily. For example, the area of a 25x15 rectangle is equivalent to the area of a 25x10 plus a 25x5. Or, it might be composed of three 25x4 rectangles and three more columns of 24. An irregular shape might be able to be split into rectangular pieces for which students can calculate the area more efficiently. This work with rectilinear shapes is an important precursor to the partitioning of a wide variety of polygons in later grades.

❖ Factoring and grouping flexibly

Factors can be associated in a variety of ways to facilitate simpler mental calculations. As children move up the grades this strategy can be very helpful. For example, 2.8 x 350 can be thought of as 28 x 35 or as 14 x 70, or as 2 x (7 x 70). Although the focus of this unit is geometry, the minilessons continue to support students to develop fluent, flexible strategies for multiplication employing the use of the associative and commutative properties.

❖ Uses generalizable perimeter formulas

Once students construct the idea that L + W can be doubled to produce the total perimeter they use it as a generalizable strategy for all rectangles: they add the length and width and double the sum [2(L+W)], or double the length and then the width and add the products [2W+2L].

❖ Uses generalizable area formulas

Once students have constructed a strong understanding of arrays—knowing that the linear unit of measure becomes a square unit when multiplied—they no longer add rows or skip-count; they multiply LxW. Note that students' computational ability also needs to be strong enough to support using multiplication-based strategies to find the area.

❖ Uses generalizable perimeter and area formulas to find unknowns

With a rectangle, if we know the area and the length of one side, we can figure out the length of the other. However, using the area formula in this way demands a deep understanding of the relationship between area and perimeter and an understanding of the inverse relationship between multiplication and division. Similarly, knowing the perimeter and the length of one side is sufficient to calculate the length of the other, but this requires an understanding of the relationship between addition and subtraction. The part/whole relationships are critical to these tasks.

One of the primary thrusts of this unit is to make use of the rectangular array model in the construction of area. The array is a powerful model for multiplicative and geometric thinking because it can support the development of the following:

- ❖ a wide range of strategies (skip-counting, repeated addition, doubling, doubling and halving, partial products) and big ideas like the distributive, associative, and commutative properties of multiplication
- ❖ visual representations of area and perimeter

Students do not automatically understand the mathematics inherent in the array, however. For the array to become a tool for thinking it should be progressively developed in three stages (Gravemeijer 1999; Fosnot and Dolk 2002):

- ❖ *model of the situation*
- ❖ *model of students' strategies*
- ❖ *model as a tool for thinking*

❖ *Model of the situation*

Models initially grow out of visual representations of a realistic situation. In this unit, the grid is used to represent the space covered inside rectangular shapes with opportunities presented for students to compose and decompose these shapes. It is important that students also be provided with opportunities to draw and defend their solutions. Number lines can be used for length and width measurements, with lines drawn from points to make rows and columns—gridded areas.

❖ *Model of students' strategies*

Students benefit from seeing the teacher model their strategies. Once a model has been introduced as a representation of the situation, you can use it to display student strategies during minilessons focused on computation. In this unit, the open array is used to model students' multiplication strategies. If a student says in solving 4 x 24, "I doubled and halved. I substituted 8 x 12," you might draw the following:

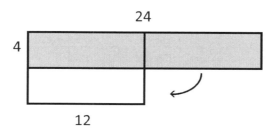

Using representations like these as you do minilessons focused on computation will give students a chance to discuss a variety of strategies they may find useful as they work on the investigations, and it will continue to support their understanding of area and perimeter.

❖ *Model as a tool for thinking*

Eventually students become able to use the array model as a tool to think with—to prove and explore their ideas about multiplicative reasoning and, more particular to this unit, as a tool to develop area and perimeter formulas. Many opportunities to use the array as a tool will arise as you work through this unit. Look for moments of puzzlement. Allowing students to decompose rectangles into sections and rearrange these sections into other arrays will help them develop area formulas. Don't hesitate to let students discuss their ideas and check and recheck their strategies. Celebrate their accomplishments! They are young mathematicians at work.

A graphic of the full landscape of learning for this unit is provided on page 5. The purpose of the graphic is to allow you to see the longer journey of students' geometric development and to place your work with *Tabletops, Floors, and Fields: Area, Perimeter, and Partitioning* within the scope of this long-term development. You may also find the graphic helpful as a way to record the progress of individual students for yourself. Each landmark can be shaded in as you find evidence in a student's work and in what the student says—evidence that a landmark strategy, big idea, or way of modeling has been constructed. In a sense, you will be recording the individual pathways your students take as they develop as young mathematicians.

References and Resources

Battista, Michael T., Doug Clements, Judy Arnoff, Kathryn Battista, and Caroline Bomsn. 1998. Students' spatial structuring of 2D arrays of squares. *Journal for Research in Mathematics Education, 29 (5)*, 503–532.

Fosnot, Catherine Twomey, and Maarten Dolk. 2002. *Young Mathematicians at Work: Constructing Multiplication and Division.* Portsmouth, NH: Heinemann.

Goodnow, Jackie. 1977. *Children Drawing*. Cambridge: Harvard University Press.

Gravemeijer, Koeno P. E. 1999. How emergent models may foster the constitution of formal mathematics. *Mathematical Thinking and Learning, 1 (2)*, 155–177.

Huang, Hsin-Mei E. and Klaus G. Witz 2011. Developing Children's Conceptual Understanding of Area Measurement. *Learning and Instruction, 21 (1)*, 1-13.

Outhred, Lynne and Michael Mitchelmore. 2004. *Students' Structuring of Rectangular Arrays.* Paper presented in the Proceedings of the 28th Conference of the International Group for the Psychology of Mathematics Education. Vol. 3, 465-472.

Piaget, Jean, Barbel Inhelder, and Anna Szeminska. 1960. *The Child's Conception of Geometry.* Translated by E.A. Lunzer, New York: Basic Books.

DAY ONE

MR. FOREST'S TABLES

Materials Needed

Mr. Forest's Tables
(Appendix A for display
and pair of students)

Pencils

**Large 1" grid chart
paper**

**Blank Chart Paper for
posters** (sticky note
style is best as it makes
taping on the walls
unnecessary)

Markers

Scissors

Glue sticks

This unit begins with the introduction of Mr. Forest, a third grade teacher, who is considering the purchase of some new classroom tables. He notes that the tables fit nicely over his floor tiles and he wonders if he could use the tiles to figure out how much working space (an equipartitioned section of the table top area) each child would have use of if four students sit at each table. Students work to generate a variety of strategies for partitioning the table area into four equal areas, providing opportunity for many rich discussions today and in the subsequent gallery walk and congress, which will be held on Day Two.

Day One Outline

Developing the Context

❖ Tell the story of Mr. Forest and his new tables.

❖ Ask students to consider how the square floor tiles might be used to determine how much workspace each of four students would have at each table.

❖ Make sure students understand that they are considering the total tabletop (not the distance along the edge) to ensure that they are not conflating area and perimeter.

Supporting the Investigation

❖ Confer with children as they work, noting the strategies they use to partition and determine area, and helping them to develop an understanding that equal partitioning splits the total area of each table with no overlaps or gaps.

❖ Support children to note that the students' areas are equivalent if the total area is partitioned fairly, even if the resulting shapes are not congruent, and encourage them to investigate why.

❖ As students finish, ask them to prepare a poster to convince others of their solutions and to share important things they have noticed along the way as they worked. These posters will be used on Day Two in a gallery walk and congress.

Developing the Context

Appendix A provides a blueprint of four table shapes shown on grid paper. The grid lines represent the square floor tiles. Gather the class in the meeting area and display Appendix A, either in paper form or projected digitally using a document camera or digital photograph of Appendix A, as you tell the following story.

> *Mr. Forest is a third grade teacher. He is ordering new tables for his classroom. He wants each table to seat four students and sees some possible options in another third grade classroom down the hall. He notices that the other classroom has the same large square tiles on the floor that his room does and he wonders if he can use that information to figure out how large the table top space is, as that is the area he knows his students will care about. They will likely all want to know exactly how much space they each get as a work area. He draws a blueprint and decides to work on the problem with his students.*

Explain that the gridlines in the picture are the floor tiles (each 1 ft by 1 ft) and that the outlines of the tables are also shown. Have a brief discussion on what students notice but only discuss these briefly to ensure they all understand the drawing. Do NOT discuss solutions. Provide a copy of Appendix A, a sheet of 1" graph paper, scissors, and pencils to each pair of students and send them off to investigate the problem.

Teacher Note: Behind the Shapes

The sizes of the shapes and their positions on the floor tiles were carefully chosen to support the development of some key big ideas and strategies on the landscape. It is important early on, as children develop ideas about area, that they explore how shapes need not be congruent to have equivalent areas. It is also important that they experience composing and decomposing of shapes and explore the effect of these actions on area. With the 2x2 and the 2x4 tables you will likely see children counting tiles or skip counting using the rows or columns. Hopefully they will also note that the 2x4 area is twice the 2x2 area. The 3x3 table provides an opportunity for them to notice how the 2x2 area fits inside the 3x3. They may even anticipate (although not asked), that a 4x4 would be twice a 2x4. If they do, they now have 3 square areas to compare (2x2, 3x3, and 4x4). These rectangular tables also provide several opportunities for children to construct the idea that the dimensions of length and width, when multiplied, produce the area and that partial products can also be added together to determine the overall area. Some students will likely think that the fourth table is equivalent to the 3x3 squares, but cutting and aligning their edges, or measuring the edges, will show this to be a false assumption. The fourth table, because it is positioned along the diagonals of the tiles has dimensions the children will not be able to produce as of yet because doing so will require the Pythagorean Theorem. This was purposeful. Do *not* try to introduce the Theorem. Instead, encourage the cutting up and rearranging of pieces to focus on the space inside. This action will provide children with opportunities to consider how shapes need not be congruent to have equivalent areas. Samples of children's work are provided in *Supporting the Investigation*.

Supporting the Investigation

As students begin to explore the different tables, make sure that all groups understand that it is the surface area of the tabletop they are measuring, not the length of the edges around the table. If some students initially talk about space in terms of how much space each student has at the *edge of each table*, conflating linear distance with area, remind them that what Mr. Forest wants to know is how much space students have *on the table*. This amount of space, or area, can be measured by how many tiles cover the space, so encourage students who are struggling to extend the outer gridlines to make gridlines within the shape. Only suggest this if it's really needed, however. The grids have not been provided within the rectangles on purpose to encourage strategies beyond simply counting squares. After extending the grid, most students will easily calculate the total area by counting the tiles inside each shape. Encourage them instead to note rows and/or columns and skip count, or to note how the 2x2 table fits inside others.

As students work to determine the space at each table, you may see some of the following strategies:

❖ Drawing curved lines to divide the space, leaving space in the middle of the table (see Figure 1.1)

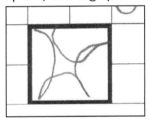

Figure 1.1

❖ Drawing gridlines, but not necessarily in reference to the outer gridlines, and counting up the resulting amount of squares (see Figure 1.2)

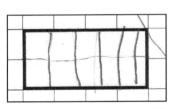 

Figure 1.2

❖ Extending the outer gridlines with precision and counting the squares within the table and partitions (see Figure 1.3)

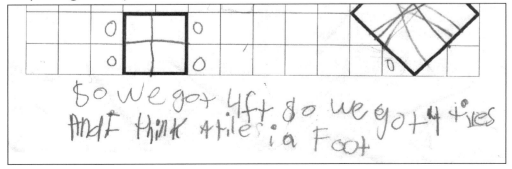

Figure 1.3

❖ Dividing the space with lines and using knowledge of the total area to determine the space for each student without recounting (see Figure 1.4)

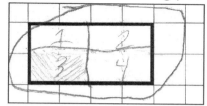 

Figure 1.4

Figures 1.1-1.4 show children's strategies for partitioning and finding the area of each student's section.

As you confer with students, encourage them to look for multiple ways to partition the entire tabletop with no empty space in the middle. If students are drawing curved lines on their diagrams, leaving empty space in the middle of each table (see Figure 1.1), use the context and ask them to whom that space belongs. You might say, "What if students want to place their books or pencils in the middle—which part belongs to which student?" Remind them that the whole tabletop is usable and must be measured and partitioned. As your students move from drawing curved lines to using straight lines that partition all the space, they are moving toward the big idea that the area of a shape is all of the space inside the outline, with no overlaps and no gaps. They are also moving towards the big idea of equal partitioning of area as they figure ways to divide the surface area of the tabletop into four equal sections, into fourths. Learners will be at different points in the landscape, so listen carefully to each partnership as you decide what questions will help support their learning.

Once they understand that area is measured precisely, with no overlaps or gaps, students will readily draw gridlines and count the tiles to calculate the entire area of each table. Students who have not yet constructed the row and column structure of grids and arrays may fill the tables with arbitrary tiles and partitions that don't align with the floor's tiles. With these groups, point to a square they have drawn and ask if it is in a row. Next, is it in a column? These questions will help students realize that gridlines have a regular pattern that you can predict and even use as a mathematical tool.

Students who do understand row and column structure will extend the gridlines with precision, and will likely count the tiles inside by ones before splitting the total area into four groups. That strategy is fine for now; larger arrays on later days will encourage students to use more efficient strategies like skip counting and multiplication. Today, these groups are ready to focus on the big idea that different shapes can have the same area, even if they are not congruent. Challenge students to show how they know that different shapes of partitions have the same area, particularly the triangular partitions of the 2x4 (see Figure 1.4).

Some partnerships may use vertical and horizontal lines to partition the area. For example see Figure 1.4, where students have partitioned the 2x4 area and have shown that each student would get 2 square tiles of space. Children who partition the 2x4 table with horizontal and vertical lines often switch to using diagonals for the other tables, either to align with the implicit partitions of the gridlines or arguing that nobody would like to sit at the corners of a table because the leg of the table would be in the way. This change in strategy was consciously supported by the context of tables. It provides you with a nice opportunity to question whether the areas are equivalent even if the resulting shapes are not congruent. Encouraging decomposition and rearranging is important. (See Figure 2.)

 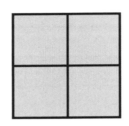 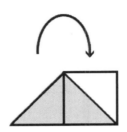

Figure 2

Of course, splitting the table from corner to corner is a natural strategy for the table aligned with the diagonals of the tiles. Once students have partitioned this table diagonally (extending the floor's gridlines), they are often able to count 1 tile plus 2 half-tiles for a total of 2 tiles per student. Many students will not realize this, however, as they will assume that this table is the same size as the 3x3 tables above it, just turned. In fact, the lengths of this table's edges are more than two tiles (the diagonal is longer than the sides of the tiles) but less than three tile sides. Students will not be able to determine the length of the diagonal line as it is not an even fraction of one side, but encourage them to cut out the shape using the graph paper to explore this table's relationship to the 3x3. The two tables have noticeably different side lengths when they are rotated and placed next to each other, and one will overlap the edges of the other. If students have extended gridlines and counted tiles, they will see that one table is 9 sq ft and the other is 8 sq ft.

The big idea that shapes can be made with other shapes is still on the horizon for most students, but the dialogue box on the following page shows a way you might support students in decomposing and recombining shapes even while they grapple with the properties of the array.

Patricia and Rick are working on the table aligned along the two diagonals. They have partitioned the shape into four equal triangular areas and have noted the gridlines mark a 2x2 square inside.

Patricia: So that's 4 tiles, but what do we do with all the other pieces?

Rick: I know. This *is* a hard one.

Becca (the teacher): How's it going with this one? It looks like you just noticed something important!

Rick: Yep. It's hard!

Becca: *(Smiling at Rick's humor)* It is! Of course that is also what makes it fun, right? A puzzle worth cracking!! What a good feeling you will have when you solve it! What I meant was what I just heard you say, Patricia. Didn't you just say there are 4 tiles in the inside, here?

Patricia: Yes. This part is like the 2x2, so we know this tabletop has more area, but now we have to figure out how to add all of the extra parts in also.

Becca: That is what I thought you said! And that is a really important noticing I think. You already know this one is bigger than the 2x2, and isn't that interesting, because it spans two tiles on each side, too. It's just that it is along this diagonal line instead of the edge. Did you think this tabletop might be the same as the 2x2 at first?

Rick: I did. And I wanted to cut it out and turn it, but then Patricia showed me that the 2x2 was already in the inside and so this had to be bigger.

Becca: Wow! So now you can see why I thought this was an important noticing. So how could we go about exploring how much more area there is here? *(Becca points to the adjacent triangles.)* I wonder if the strategy you just used, when you find a piece inside that you know, would be helpful again.

Author's notes

Becca moves around the room, noting the strategies being used, and then sits to confer with a few groups as they work.

She starts the conferral by listening intently first and noting the strategy the children are using. Note how she states that challenging problems are the ones worth doing. This encourages a positive growth mindset and the willingness to persevere—one of the important standards of mathematical practice. Then she supports by celebrating the strategy of decomposing that she sees them using.

Becca mentors by clarifying and pointing out the importance of their strategy. Then she supports them to consider how it might be helpful to use again. This move "ups the ante," but in a very supportive way. The role of the teacher is not to just facilitate; it is to mentor.

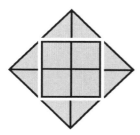

Rick: I think the triangles have 2 smaller triangles in them and 2 of the triangles make a square. Each kid is going to have half of the 2x2, I think..... Each kid gets an area the size of two tiles?

Patricia: Oh yeah! You are right! It is one whole tile and 2 halves! So the whole area must be 8 tiles and then each kid gets two square feet.

Becca: Wow. This is so exciting what you are doing. Why don't you get scissors and cut the pieces up to show everyone how you thought about this? We are going to have a gallery walk and congress tomorrow and this idea would be really helpful to share. Do you think you could make your poster about this, about your idea of using shapes within shapes and cutting and rearranging pieces to make new shapes you know to figure out the area?

The two students are now composing and decomposing to produce equivalent areas. This will be an important discussion in the congress tomorrow.

As she leaves to confer with other pairs at work, Becca urges Patricia and Rick to make a poster to prove that the areas are equivalent, even though they aren't congruent—an important idea on the landscape of learning for geometry, and an idea that will be an important focus in the congress tomorrow.

As students begin to reach conclusions about how much area each student would receive at each table, ask them to prepare posters presenting their findings for a gallery walk and congress on Day Two. Explain that mathematicians often want to share their findings with each other, and that when they do they are careful to choose the most important ideas to share. As students prepare their work on poster paper, they should not copy every step they took. Instead, encourage students to record how their thinking changed, the interesting connections they noticed, and the arguments they used to convince each other that their answers were correct. What was the area of each table? How much of the total area does each student get? If the partitions aren't congruent how do we know they are equivalent? How can we be sure we have included everything fairly with no gaps or overlaps? Many students will also be ready to answer a fifth question: Is there more than one way to split a table fairly?

Reflections on the Day

Today students were asked to measure area, partition a rectangle into equal parts, and justify their reasoning. As area is a new concept for many students in third grade, you likely saw a wide range of strategies as students grappled with the idea that they can measure, and partition, space. Note whether any of your students saw partitions as related to fractions or used language like "they each get a quarter of the table." You may be able to use the ideas or language from these groups to initiate a conversation about the relationship between fair-sharing and describing a region as a fraction of a whole. Day Two's congress will provide an opportunity for a rich discussion about area and partitioning as students explain how they know they covered all of the space on the table and which table has the most space for each of four students.

DAY TWO

COMPARING THE TABLES

Materials Needed

Students' work from Day One

Large chart paper prepared with quadrilateral definition

Smaller paper prepared with rectangle definition

Sorting Quadrilaterals (Two cut-out copies of the shapes in Appendix B)

Today begins with a minilesson in order to support students' understanding of how 2-D shapes can be categorized and sorted. By determining if certain shapes fit or do not fit each category and if one category fits into another, students grapple with the big idea of class inclusion: in this particular case that all rectangles are also quadrilaterals and that a square is also a rectangle. Class inclusion will continue to be developed throughout the unit, coming up again on Day Four. After the minilesson, students put finishing touches to their posters from Day One and share their work in a gallery walk. Then they return to the meeting area for a math congress to discuss a few of the work samples more deeply.

Day Two Outline

Minilesson: Sorting Quadrilaterals
❖ Students learn the definition of a quadrilateral and sort shapes into and out of the quadrilateral group. Next they sort shapes into/out of a group of rectangles, and then determine whether the rectangle group itself can be placed in the quadrilateral category.

Facilitating the Gallery Walk
❖ Conduct a gallery walk to allow students time to reflect and comment on each other's posters from Day One.

Facilitating the Math Congress
❖ Convene students at the meeting area to discuss a few important ideas about area that arose during the investigation on Day One.

Minilesson: Sorting Quadrilaterals

Begin Math Workshop by asking students to reflect on the shapes of the tabletops that they have been exploring. Ask them to consider what the shapes have in common. As students generate ideas such as all of the tabletops are four-sided, have straight sides, have four angles (or corners), etc., bring their attention to a large piece of chart paper you prepared in advance with the definition of a quadrilateral: "A quadrilateral is a four-sided, closed shape with straight lines as sides." Draw a large circle below the quadrilateral definition and ask students which shapes would be contained in a group of quadrilaterals. Provide cutouts of the shapes in Appendix B and ask which of these shapes belong in the group of quadrilaterals. As students discuss and come to agreement on which shapes belong in the category, place them inside or outside of the circle using tape or magnets.

Next turn to a second piece of paper with the definition of a rectangle: "A rectangle is a closed shape with four straight sides and four right angles." As before, provide new copies of the shapes in Appendix B and ask which of these shapes belong in the group of rectangles. As students become comfortable placing shapes inside or outside the rectangle groups, some may notice that the rectangle and square are in both the quadrilateral and rectangle categories. At this point, ask the class to consider if this is part of a larger pattern. Will all rectangles fit inside the quadrilateral circle? Will there be some that don't? Ultimately, discuss whether you can place the whole rectangle group within the group of quadrilaterals.

Students are now considering one of the big ideas of this unit: class inclusion. All rectangles must be quadrilaterals by definition. In order to be a rectangle, a shape has to have four sides and must therefore be a quadrilateral. [Note: A square is a rectangle (the regular form where the side lengths are all equal) and is also a quadrilateral.] The big idea here is that one shape can belong to more than one group of shapes. Some children may be able to see this quickly; others will need much more discussion and reflection in order to construct this logic and generalize it to multiple categories. Thus, class inclusion will be revisited again and again as the unit progresses.

Teacher Note

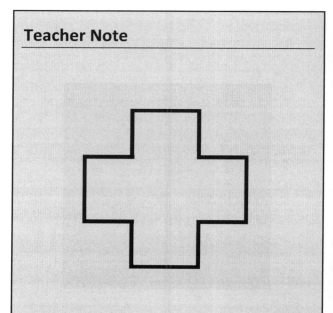

Some students who seem quite comfortable identifying most quadrilaterals may also think that the plus-sign is a quadrilateral. These students are comparing their visual impression of the shape (the four outermost sides) with the squares and rectangles they have seen over the years rather than analyzing the plus-sign based on its Euclidean properties of twelve sides and twelve turns. This is a nice opportunity to facilitate a discussion on the properties mathematicians use to categorize shapes, beginning with the number of sides and turns and, with rectangles, the size of the angles.

Facilitating the Gallery Walk

Ask students to return to the posters they began on Day One, adding any finishing touches they desire, and then to post their work around the room for a gallery walk. Depending on how much prior experience your students have had doing gallery walks, it may be helpful to provide instructions before you pass out the sticky notes. If your students have not done a gallery walk for some time, or if you think they need more instruction on how to proceed, see the Teacher Note section below.

> ### Teacher Note
>
> Let your students know that their comments and questions should be specific about the math on the poster, and to steer clear of comments such as "Good job!" or "I like your poster." Remind students that specific comments and questions are most helpful. In this context, students might say "I'm not convinced that when you drew the diagonals the pieces were the same size. I need more explanation," or "I like that you show two different ways." It may help to give the example of writing workshop, since most students can remember a time when a peer said something like, "I like your story!" but was not specific. Once you have gone over a few examples and perhaps even modeled writing a comment or question, pass out the sticky notes. Explain that you are going to start by passing out three sticky notes, and students can return to get more if needed.

Ask students to start at different places and give each a few sticky notes, enough so that after about 10 minutes, all posters will have at least a few comments. Remind students that gallery walks should be quiet times so that all reviewers can read and think before commenting. This time should be taken seriously. One of the Standards of Mathematical Practice is to read and write viable arguments and this is a time to foster the development of that ability.

After the gallery walk, invite the groups to go back to their posters to see what comments and questions were left for them. Allow a few minutes for everyone to think about the feedback they received and to discuss any new ideas with their partners before convening the whole class in the meeting area for a congress.

Facilitating the Math Congress

Review the posters and choose a few that you can use for a discussion that will deepen understanding and support growth along the landscape of learning described in the overview. For example, if you had some students who extended the grid lines and counted the tiles by ones, you might start with them and use the congress to foster more efficient strategies like skip counting or using partial products (the area of a smaller tabletop within another).

If several of your students skip counted, you might have a student share who noticed that the area of the 2x4 table is double the area of the 2x2. Others might be able to share that the 3x3 has just one more square than the 2x4. Cutting a column of two tiles off of the 2x4 and moving it under the remaining 2x3 piece might support others to notice this relationship. The relationship between the 2x2 and 3x3 tables can also foster rich discussion.

Perhaps most students seem comfortable partitioning the tables, but there is some disagreement as to whether you can equally partition the tabletops in more than one way. In this case the congress is a good opportunity to discuss how the partitioning provided each of the 4 students with ¼ of the total area of that particular table. Different groups might have partitions that are congruent to each other, but different from other groups' pieces, and some groups might even have partitioned a table into pieces that are equivalent but not congruent, particularly the 2x4 table. Invite a few pairs to show how they proved that the pieces were equivalent.

A discussion on the table aligned along the diagonal of two tiles will provide another opportunity to discuss congruence and equivalence. Invite discussion on strategies used to determine the area of this table. For example, if some students have cut triangular fourths and moved two of them to make two whole tiles, promote discussion on how it is that this table, although a different shape, has the same area as the 2x4 table.

Inside One Classroom: A Portion of the Congress

Julio and Crystal have cut out a 2x4 table and drawn vertical and horizontal lines to show the partitioning. With the 2x2 table they have changed their strategy and drawn diagonals to produce 4 equal triangular areas.

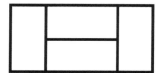

Becca has asked them to start the congress by sharing their strategies and what they noticed. Throughout the discussion, Becca and her students say "2x4" as "2 by 4."

Julio: The 2x4 table takes 8 tiles to cover the top. We know that because it has 2 rows of 4, and 4 + 4 is 8.

Becca (the teacher): Before you go any further Julio….you just said a big thing there and I want everyone to have a chance to talk about it. You said the 2x4 table has 2 rows of 4 tiles, so the area is 2 fours, and that sounds like multiplication to me. Is this 8 square feet? Could we just multiply 2 feet by 4 feet? Let's all turn and talk about this to a partner. *(As the children engage in pair talk, Becca listens in and then supports further whole group discussion.)* Pablo and Diana, you seem to agree that it is multiplication. Could you tell us why?

Author's notes

Becca invites Julio and Crystal to share first. Their poster will provide for a rich conversation on the ideas of decomposition and equivalence of area, as well as an opportunity to notice that the area of the 2x4 is double the area of the 2x2. Her plan is to then build on these ideas with the poster of Patricia and Rick (see the dialogue box from Day One). This pair will defend how the area of the table along the diagonals of the tiles has an area equal to the 2x4; shapes can have equal area even if they are not congruent.

As Julio shares, Becca can't help but stop even though it is a sidetrack from her plan for the congress. It is an important moment not to miss, and she attempts to support a shift from addition to multiplicative structuring. She knows this will be a big

Pablo: (excitedly) It is! We didn't see it before, but it is 2 fours. And the 2x2 is 2 twos; and the 3x3 is 3 threes.

Diana: And the tile is 1 foot by 1 foot.

Becca: Wow. You have given us a lot to think about here, Julio and Crystal. Let's keep this idea in mind over the next couple of weeks as we work on some further investigations and see if multiplication continues to be helpful. I'll write this down so we don't forget about it, but for now let's have you continue with what you started to explain on your poster.

Crystal: We've got our strategies all drawn on the poster. So for the 2x4 table each kid would get 2 tiles of area. We cut the 2x2 up differently. We drew our lines like this (she points to the diagonals), but we knew the 2x2 was half of the 2x4 because we could see that two of them fit on the 2x4.

Pablo: Right, so then we knew the area each kid would get here is half, so it must be just 1 tile.

Becca: How many people can put in their own words what Crystal and Pablo are doing? (Noting that not many hands go up, she suggests pair talk again.) Turn and talk about this with a partner.

shift for some, so she provides pair talk for reflection and small group discussion, and then steers the group back to focus on decomposition and equivalent areas.

Becca does not attempt to get everyone to understand how linear units of distance become square units of area, since this is only Day Two of the unit. Multiplication will surface again as a focus as the class continues with the unit.

As Becca continues to facilitate the conversation in the congress, note how she makes use of pair talk and paraphrasing. If children cannot put in their own words what is being discussed, there is no use going on as many will be lost. Providing pair talk at moments like this not only reengages children, it also provides important reflection time for learning.

Reflections on the Day

Math workshop began today with a minilesson where students sorted 2-D shapes by their properties and grappled with class inclusion of squares, rectangles, and quadrilaterals. By participating in a gallery walk on their work from Day One, students had opportunities to read and write viable arguments and then consider their classmates' comments, questions, and suggestions. Opportunities like these are designed to support the development of proof-making. A math congress provided opportunities for further discussion and reflection on the topic of conservation of area. Students developed strategies to find the area of each table and to partition each table into four equal parts. They also likely discovered that the area of each table is composed of the amount of square tiles that cover the space, that there is more than one way to partition the tables equally, and that areas can be equivalent without shapes needing to be congruent. Tomorrow, students will build on today's understandings of area as they calculate the area of larger rectangles and are introduced to a new measurement: perimeter.

DAY THREE

COMPARING CLASSROOMS

Materials Needed

Comparing Classrooms
(Both pages of
Appendix C for each
pair of students)

Pencils

**Large paper with 1"
grid**

Markers

Rulers or straight-edges

$\mathbb{T}$oday the investigation shifts from area alone to a comparison of area and perimeter. Given grid outlines, students determine strategies to find the area and perimeter of two different classrooms, one 20x20 and the other 15x25. Many students will likely be surprised to discover that although the distance around each classroom is the same, the areas inside are different. Where did the extra area go?

Day Three Outline

Minilesson: Partial Products
❖ A string of related problems is used to support students to begin to use partial products. Strategies are represented on an open array model to engender insights related to area.

Developing the Context
❖ Mr. Forest and his colleague, Ms. Suarez, disagree about the size of their two classrooms. Is one classroom bigger? Ms. Suarez is thinking about the space inside the rooms—the area covered with tiles. Mr. Forest is thinking about the distance around the outside of the floor space, along the walls—the perimeter of the room.
❖ As you develop the context use the words area and perimeter naturally, as part of the story. Don't try to define terms upfront, just make the terms a natural part of the story, and continue to use the words in context as you confer.

Supporting the Investigation
❖ Note students' strategies as they work to find the perimeter and area. Support their growth along the landscape as they shift from counting strategies to more multiplicative thinking.
❖ Students will notice that the two perimeters are the same, while the areas are different. Encourage them to investigate why this might be.

Minilesson: A string of related problems (10-15 minutes)

Begin Math Workshop by gathering students at the meeting area for a minilesson. Explain that you will write one problem at a time and give them "think time." They should let you know with a "thumbs up" when they are ready to respond. Monitor the thumbs to judge when discussion should occur. When problems are difficult (you'll be able to tell from the thumbs), provide pair talk for reflection and discussion before starting whole group discussion. Move around and listen to some of the discussions to help you understand students' challenges, then start whole group discussion. As students share their strategies, model their thinking using an open array. If this representation is new for you a dialogue box is provided to help you. As you progress through the string, you can name strategies after the children who invent them and begin a classroom "strategy wall." In third grade, the formal terms of the properties are usually not needed, but follow the guidelines of your own state standards.

The string:

10 x 5

5 x 5

15 x 5

15 x 2

10 x 2

5 x 2

5 x 20

15 x 20

15 x 25

> ## Behind the Numbers
>
> Most students will either skip count or use a place value pattern they have made note of previously and "add a zero after the 5" to produce 50. As you draw an array to represent the 10 rows of 5, point out that 5 is now in the tens place and ask students to look for the 5 tens in the array. [They are in the columns.] This discussion provides an opportunity to write 10x5 = 5x10. It is the commutative property (along with the place value) that explains why the pattern when multiplying by ten happens, and the array can be turned 90 degrees to represent the commutative property. The second problem is equal to half of the first. It is also a fact many students are likely to know. 15x5 is the sum of 10x5 and 5x5, encouraging the use of the distributive property and partial products. Some students will likely not notice this relationship and will skip count, but some may notice it, and this will provide for a rich discussion. 15x2 can be solved by skip counting by twos, but some might see it as 2x15 (a double), and the array can once again be used to represent the commutative property. The next two problems provide a place to revisit partial products: 15x2 = 10x2 + 5x2. The next problem, 5x20, will likely be solved as 5x10 + 5x10, but others may see it as 5x2 ten times. This provides a chance to write 5x20 = 5x(10x2) = (5x10)x2 = (5x2)x10. Encourage children to notice that order and association don't seem to matter when multiplying. Doing so lays the foundation for later work when the properties are generalized. Students may use these properties to help them with 15x20 as well. The final challenge problem to end this string offers children opportunities to consider the best attack and decompose in their own personal ways. Continue using the array to represent student strategies throughout the string.

Becca (the teacher): So this first problem was easy for most of you. Let me draw a picture of it as an area, sort of like our tabletops from the other day. Here are 10 rows of 5 tiles. And you said the area was 50, so I'll write that in the middle of the shape. I'm curious. A lot of you said you just knew to put a zero after the 5. Do you know why that works? Now the 5 is in the tens place, so we have 5 tens. Can you find them in this picture? Turn to a partner and talk about this.

Becca: *(As the children talk, Becca moves around and listens to some of the conversations. After a few moments, she starts whole group discussion.)* Cael, I saw you and Claude using your hands and turning them. Start us off. What were you talking about?

Cael: Claude and I were saying that the tens are in the columns, but it is like the tabletop. You can turn it to make it 5 rows of 10. The area is the same. The table just got turned.

Becca: Oh, that is interesting, isn't it! So can I write this to represent your thinking? *(She draws the array turned 90 degrees to show 5 rows of 10, and writes 10x5 = 5x10.)* Is this what you mean? The order doesn't matter, because it is the same tabletop, just turned? Wow! Does this always work when we multiply? Can we just turn the shape if it makes it easier? Turn and talk about this again. If we all agree, we'll get it up on our strategy wall and name this idea after Cael and Claude!

(After some further discussion and agreement, Becca writes down the next problem, 5x5, which all of her children know. She quickly adds a picture of that array, and then writes 15x5. She notes that many of her students are using their fingers to keep track of the skip counting they are doing and decides to have some pair talk before the whole group discussion.)

Becca: Turn and talk to a partner. See if the strategy your

Author's notes

Becca provides time for pair talk as a way to push reflection on the commutative property—how the factors have been reordered. She uses the array to represent her children's thinking. During the pair talk she moves around and listens to several discussions to determine her next move.

Becca has succeeded in getting the commutative property up for discussion and now as the string continues, it can be examined further.

By using the open array as a representational tool and building a connection to the tabletop areas, Becca supports students to visualize how the parts are moved without changing the area.

partner is using is the same or different than yours. (*After a few minutes she resumes whole group discussion.*) Did anyone have an interesting partner…someone who gave you a good idea?

Christina: Mateo was my partner. He had a great idea. He said I didn't have to do all of the skip counting because I already know what 10x5 is.

Becca: (*Writes 10x5 and draws the array.*) Wow! I can see why you thought he was interesting! That saved a lot of time, didn't it! What did you do next, Mateo?

Mateo: Then I added 25, because that was 5 rows more, and that was 15 rows altogether.

Becca: Wow. Let me make a picture of that. We'll get that up on our strategy wall, too. Mateo's strategy: use pieces (partial products) that you know and put them together! (*Becca draws the pieces under discussion using two connected open arrays.*)

By asking if anyone had a helpful partner, Becca is implicitly communicating that during pair talk each and every student should try to be an interesting and helpful partner. Talk must be "accountable talk" in a community of mathematicians at work.

Strategies are named after the mathematicians who invented them. Over the course of the year students will make use of one another's strategies and build further ideas on them.

Developing the Context

After finishing the minilesson, introduce the story of Mr. Forest and Ms. Suarez, the art teacher, explaining the following while displaying Appendix C1 and C2:

Mr. Forest and the art teacher, Ms. Suarez, have been chatting in the teacher's lounge. Ms. Suarez is thinking about arranging her art tables into new shapes, but she doesn't think she has as much space as Mr. Forest has in his classroom. Mr. Forest disagrees.

"Your room is just as big," he says. "I remember walking all around the edges when we hung up the students' pictures, and I'm sure it was the same distance around each room."

"That can't be right!" says Ms. Suarez. "You all just have so much more space upstairs. The rooms look much larger and I'm sure there are more tiles needed to cover the floor's area."

Can you help the teachers figure out if their classrooms are different sizes? Here is a drawing, a blueprint of Mr. Forest's room without any furniture in it. His room is 20 feet long and 20 feet wide. The Art Room is a different shape: it is 25 feet long and 15 feet wide. With your partner, find the area (the number of tiles that fit inside) and the perimeter (the distance around all the sides) of each room. Are the classrooms different sizes? How do you know?

Pass out a copy of Appendix C1 and C2 to each student. Remind the students that they are trying to find two different measurements. The perimeter, the total distance of the sides, along the edges of the room, is a measurement of **how far** or **how long** a line is—how many feet long the distance is. The area, on the other hand, is a measurement of **how many** tiles or **how much** space the floor of each classroom takes up, and this is measured in square feet.

Supporting the Investigation

As students begin to explore the grids of the two classrooms, make sure that all groups are differentiating between the space inside and the distance around each classroom. If necessary, remind students that the perimeter is how far Mr. Forest would have to walk to go around the sides of each room. This distance is measurement along a line, or really along several straight lines joined by turns. The area, on the other hand, is a measurement of space just like the space students measured on the tables in Days One and Two. The perimeter will be a number of (linear) feet and the area will be a number of "tiles," which are each worth one square foot in this investigation. As students improvise terminology, make sure that area terms like "tiles" and "squares" are clearly differentiated from distance terms like "feet" or "lines."

As students work to determine the area you may see some of the following strategies:
   ❖ Counting the tiles by ones, marking them off in a spiral pattern or back and forth
   ❖ Counting some squares twice, not coordinating rows and columns
   ❖ Counting by ones using the grid structure, moving in rows or columns
   ❖ Skip-counting by a friendly number such as 5 or 10
   ❖ Skip-counting by the value of an entire row or column
   ❖ Multiplying to find the area of subdivisions using partial products
   ❖ Using 10 times, employing the commutative property and place value patterns to multiply the side lengths

---

Teacher Note

The perimeter calculations in this investigation are relatively simple, and imagining the two teachers walking around the edges of each classroom will probably be enough support for students who are unsure. For a more thorough description of perimeter strategies, see Day Five.

As you confer with students, encourage them to look for efficient strategies. As students move from counting by ones to using the row and column structure of a grid to guide their skip-counting or partial products, they are moving toward the big idea that each square is in a row and column simultaneously. **However, do not suggest that students simply multiply the two side lengths.** This big idea is still on the horizon for most learners, and you want students to come to this realization on their own, after first mathematizing the grid structure and its organization in rows and columns. There will be many opportunities for students to develop this understanding over the coming week and a half. If some students are using counting you might suggest they think about the minilesson and ask if there are any partial products they already know and could use to make their work more efficient. For students who are using the ten times product along with other partial products, support them to generalize the commutative and distributive properties by asking if these strategies can always be used for multiplication. Encourage them to build an argument as to why these properties are generalizable.

As students finish their calculations, many students will be surprised to find that, although the perimeters of the two classrooms are the same, the area is different. Area and perimeter are related, but they do not have a direct correlation. Understanding that area may vary even while perimeter remains constant is an important big idea in today's investigation. At first, students may think that their answers are incorrect and revisit their work to check. This verification can be a valuable opportunity to ask students to justify their work. Using the large grid paper, ask students to prepare posters presenting their findings for a gallery walk and congress on Day Four. What is the area of each classroom? What is the perimeter? How can you be sure you have included everything with no gaps or overlaps, and where did the extra area go?

Teacher Note

The 20x20 classroom is a square with an area of 400 square feet. The Art Room, on the other hand, is 15x25. Since the perimeter remained constant—the length taken from one side was added to the adjacent side—the relationship of the two areas can be seen in the difference of two squares. Area = $(x+y)(x-y) = x^2-y^2$. The area is, in fact, $20^2 - 5^2$. This relationship can also be modeled with an array.

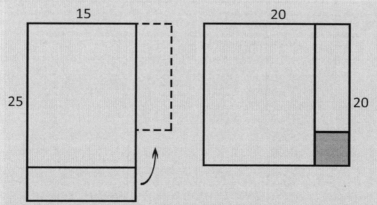

If the extra portion is cut from the bottom of the 15x25 array and rotated to the side, it is not long enough to complete a 20x20 square. The missing piece is a 5x5 square.

Reflections on the Day

Today students were asked to transfer their understanding of area to a new context with larger values. They also calculated perimeter, and explored the relationship between two rectangles with the same perimeter. It's likely that many students are still puzzled that the areas of both rectangles were not the same; this disequilibrium will provide a foundation for rich discussion in the gallery walk and congress on Day Four.

DAY FOUR

THE MISSING TILES

Materials Needed

Students' work from Day Three

Large chart paper prepared with polygon definition

Smaller paper prepared with triangle definition

Sorting Polygons and Triangles (cut-out shapes from Appendix D)

Math Workshop begins today with a minilesson introducing the definition of a simple polygon and a triangle. Students determine which shapes belong in each class and grapple with the big idea of class inclusion: all triangles are also polygons. Following the minilesson students add finishing touches to their posters started on Day Three. A subsequent gallery walk and a math congress ensue, where strategies to find the area of a larger space and insights regarding the relationship between area and perimeter of rectangles are the focus.

Day Four Outline

Minilesson: Sorting Polygons and Triangles

❖ Students learn the definition of a polygon and sort shapes into/out of the polygon group.

❖ Students sort shapes into/out of a triangle group, and then determine whether the triangle group itself can be placed inside of/outside of the polygon category.

Facilitating the Gallery Walk

❖ Conduct a gallery walk to allow students time to reflect and comment on each other's posters.

Facilitating the Math Congress

❖ Convene students at the meeting area to discuss a few important ideas on the landscape, including the relationship between area and perimeter.

Minilesson: Sorting Polygons

Display a large piece of chart paper prepared with the definition of a polygon: "A polygon is a closed shape with straight lines as sides." Draw a large circle below this definition. On the side display the cut-out shapes from the first page of Appendix D. Ask students which shapes belong inside the polygon group.

When students have placed those shapes, turn to a second (smaller) piece of paper with the definition of a triangle: "A triangle is a closed shape with three straight sides." Provide cut-outs of the shapes on the second page of Appendix D and ask which shapes belong in the triangle group. Some of the shapes will be repeated and some new; this is intentional to allow students to make connections between the two groups.

Once all students seem comfortable placing shapes inside or outside the polygon and triangle groups, ask the class to ponder a new question: could we place the whole triangle group on the polygon paper? Cut around the circle containing the set of triangles and ask students where you should place it.

As students debate the placement of the set of triangles, they are continuing to grapple with the big idea of class inclusion. All triangles must be polygons by definition, because the triangle class is a subset of the polygon class. In order to be a triangle, a shape must be closed with (three) straight sides, fulfilling the definition of the polygon class as well. Just as it can be challenging for children to recognize that a square also has the properties of a rectangle (and a quadrilateral and a polygon), and may be correctly called by those names, it is a big shift for students to think of a triangular polygon as belonging to two groups at once.

Many children will recognize that all of the shapes in the triangle category are also polygons. But does this mean that all possible triangles will also be polygons? As you facilitate the discussion, listen for children who argue that any possible triangle will also belong in the set of polygons. These students are developing a robust understanding of class membership and the properties of a triangle and polygon. Other children may believe that you need to test each new triangle, and will need to participate in several more discussions before they are able to generalize their understanding to make judgments about whole categories of shapes. The conversations in this unit will continue to provide these students with opportunities to shift and stretch their understanding.

Teacher Note

If most students are in the early stages of poster work, it can seem premature to hold a gallery walk and congress. You can start by providing everyone with more work time, but you can also hold a gallery walk on students' early work. Explain that no one is finished and that students are not commenting on final work, but rather on other groups' starting ideas. A gallery walk with this structure can help cross-pollinate ideas between partnerships and re-energize groups to return to work on their posters before a math congress occurs.

Facilitating the Gallery Walk

Provide students with time to add finishing touches to the posters they began yesterday and then have them display the posters around the classroom for other groups to view. Give students only a few sticky notes, so they have to think carefully about where they will place them. Have students walk around and read a few of the posters silently for 5-10 minutes, making sure that every poster gets read by a least a few children and that every poster gets at least a few sticky notes.

After the gallery walk, invite the groups to return to their posters to see what comments were left. Allow students a few minutes to think about this feedback and any new ideas they now have. Provide time for a short discussion with partners before convening the whole class in the meeting area.

Facilitating the Math Congress

After Day Three, review the students' work. Note the strategies used and look for evidence of big ideas that will help you structure the congress. Review the landscape in the Overview and consider how a congress could benefit each child. The congress is not a place to discuss one intended outcome for all; it is a place for a discussion that can support development of all of your students, but in different ways. If a child has drawn a grid and struggled to coordinate rows and columns, perhaps he leaves the congress having a better idea of how a square is in both a row and a column simultaneously. For those that counted by ones, can the congress be used to promote and support skip counting? For those using addition strategies to calculate perimeter and area, can the congress be instrumental in fostering multiplicative structuring of formulas for rectangles, for example seeing that $P = 2 \times (L+W)$ and $A = L \times W$? Part of the congress time should be used to foster progressive development of students' strategies.

A second focus of the congress should be the big idea that shapes can have the same perimeter yet have different areas. Students are usually fascinated by the "missing" area in the Art Room and benefit from a rich conversation in congress discussing the relationship between area and perimeter and where the "hole" came from. Find posters that can be used as explanation, perhaps showing the decomposition and rearranging of the area and the resulting hole.

Figures 3 and 4 on the next page show two examples of student work. The first group is just beginning to take advantage of the row structure to skip count by entire rows. (Notice how they discovered vertical patterns in their counting before realizing they didn't need to write all the numbers!) The second group is in a very different part of the landscape and multiplied each rectangle's dimensions without even showing the rows and columns. The following dialogue box shows how Becca used these two pieces of work in a portion of her math congress.

Figure 3 - Christina and Daniel's work

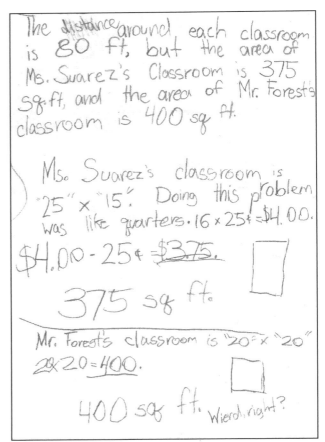

The distance around each classroom is 80 ft, but the area of Ms. Suarez's Classroom is 375 sq ft, and the area of Mr. Forest's classroom is 400 sq ft.

Ms. Suarez's classroom is "25" x "15". Doing this problem was like quarters. 16 x 25¢ = $4.00.

$4.00 - 25¢ = $3.75.

375 sq ft.

Mr. Forest's classroom is "20" x "20"

20 x 20 = 400.

400 sq ft. Wierd, right?

Figure 4 - Charlie and Nova's work

Inside One Classroom: A Portion of the Minilesson

Christina: So we started counting by twos because it was a lot of boxes. We got up to 60, and then we noticed that the ends of the rows were 20, 40, 60, and then we predicted it would be 80.

Daniel: Yeah. We checked up to 120, and after that we just used 20 for each row because they're all the same.

Becca: That made a huge difference, didn't it? You can be much more efficient if each row is the same! Did anybody else use that strategy?

Jon: Yeah, we did. We saw it was 20 across one row so we counted by 20s going down and we got 400. And then we checked the other way, and we got 400 too.

Daniel: Us too. In the Art Room it was easier up and down so we counted by 25s and we only got to 375. So it's smaller.

Author's notes

Becca starts with this group because she hopes their path from counting by ones to skip counting will engage other students who used counting strategies.

Becca: Interesting! So a couple of groups used a skip counting strategy taking advantage of the rows going across or the columns going down? I wonder, can we always do that? Turn and talk with a partner about this idea. *(Becca circulates, listening, and then brings the group back together.)* I'm hearing most of you sounding pretty convinced. Can anyone share what convinced you?

Cael: The rows never changed! We were going around in circles and each circle got smaller but it's straight across and the rows stay the same. This way makes it way easier!

Becca: Thanks for sharing that great strategy, Christina and Daniel! And now I also want us to talk about how Nova and Charlie tackled this one. *(Becca has Nova and Charlie's poster ready and places it on the board while they come up front.)*

Nova: Well, we multiplied and knew twenty 20s was 400. When we saw the 25s we thought about money. Four quarters is a dollar, so 16 rows would be $4.00, but we only had 15 so we took away 25 cents and got 375.

Becca: Whoa, that was a lot! Let me see if I can draw a picture of what you're saying to help us understand your strategy better. You said you're doing multiplication here?

Charlie: Yeah.

Becca: So I'm hearing that you needed fifteen 25s so you used four 25s to help you. *(She draws the open array below left.)*

You were thinking about this like 15 times 25, and so you split it into 4 rows, then 4 more and 4 more? *(Nova and Charlie nod.)*

Charlie: But the last group was only 3, so we took away 25. *(Becca removes the last row as shown on the right.)* Yeah, like that. You could have counted up three 25s, too. It's 375.

Becca takes a moment to make sure all students consider this important structuring of the array into rows and columns.

Charlie and Nova used multiplication without any counting or gridlines. This is a big leap from the previous poster. Because they used money, however, Nova and Charlie have implicitly used 4x25=100 as a partial product. Becca draws an open array to help other students see the connection between this group's multiplicative reasoning and the original rectangle. When the third group shares another partial product strategy, students will now have an example to help them connect area strategies with the multiplication strings they have done with open arrays.

Reflections on the Day

In Math Workshop today, students had the opportunity to share and read each other's mathematical work on the size of two classrooms with similar perimeters but different areas. A gallery walk and math congress provided opportunities for students to develop more efficient strategies to calculate area and perimeter and to explore the relationship between the two measurements. A minilesson continuing the categorization work from Day Two focused students' attention on a different aspect of shapes: the properties of polygons and triangles. Tomorrow, students' understanding will be challenged as they consider irregular polygons composed of rectangular shapes and work on finding the area and perimeter of groups of tables that Ms. Suarez has pushed together in the Art Room.

DAY FIVE

IN THE ART ROOM

Materials Needed

Ms. Suarez's Art Tables (Appendix E, one per pair of children)

Ms. Suarez's New Table Designs (Appendix F, one per pair of children)

Chart size 1" graph paper for posters

Pencils

Markers

Scissors

Glue sticks

Today begins with a new context: Ms. Suarez's art classroom. Students are told that Ms. Suarez has heard about Mr. Forest's tables and is now wondering about her own. There are many different sizes of rectangular tables in the art room and Ms. Suarez wants to know the area and perimeter of each of her tables and what the new area and perimeters will be when she pushes some of the tables together to make larger workspaces.

The context of pushing tables together to create larger workspaces provides students with opportunities to generate a variety of strategies for composing and recombining shapes to find the total area, as well as to grapple with what happens to interior edges when shapes are joined. A math congress on this work, held on Day Six, will allow students to discuss and further develop these big ideas.

Day Five Outline

Developing the Context

❖ Explain to students that Ms. Suarez needs help determining the area and perimeter of the tables in the art room.

❖ When Ms. Suarez pushes the tables together to accommodate a new art project, what are the perimeters and areas of the newly constructed tabletops?

Supporting the Investigation

❖ Move around and confer with students as they work, noting the strategies they are using, celebrating their new ideas, and challenging as appropriate as they work to find the areas and perimeters of these new tables.

Developing the Context

Gather the class in the meeting area and display Appendix E, either from the book or by projecting the image with a document camera or similar tool. Introduce the story of Ms. Suarez's tables, explaining the following:

Ms. Suarez hears Mr. Forest talking in the faculty lounge about how his students helped him choose new tables for his classroom. Ms. Suarez wonders how much table space she has in her art room. She often covers her tables with butcher block paper to protect them because many of her projects are messy. She tapes along the edges—all along the perimeter—to hold the paper down. (Display Appendix E). So, Ms. Suarez wants to know the perimeter and the area of each table.

She was also planning to do a new mural project on the floor, but she wonders if the tables could be combined so that sections of the mural could be done at a few larger tables! What would the area of these new tables be and what is the total distance around the edges of these new tables? (Display Appendix F).

Pass out a copy of Appendix E to each pair of students and provide them with several sheets of graph paper. Remind students that they are trying to find both the workspace of each tabletop—the area, and the distance around the edge of each table where the tape will go—the perimeter.

Ask students to work on Appendix E first and to come take a copy of Appendix F when they finish. Working on the original tables first ensures that students will have opportunities to predict what will happen to the area and perimeter when tables are combined.

Supporting the Investigation

As students begin to explore the different table areas, look for movement along the landscape. Some students may still be counting each square individually, even after Days Three and Four of the unit, when larger areas necessitated the use of multiplicative strategies. The grid lines are purposefully not drawn in to encourage students to use higher level strategies than just counting. It is possible that some may still need to draw in the lines, however, particularly if they still have not constructed the idea that a square is in both a row and a column simultaneously.

Other students will be able to visualize tiles in groups at this point, and therefore may have no need for extending the outer gridlines. Drawing the entire set of grid lines will only allow for counting—a backwards movement in development—so don't encourage it. Hopefully, most of your students are skip counting or multiplying by now. If not, this is another opportunity for them to develop these strategies.

As students measure the perimeters, you may see some of the following strategies:

❖ Counting the squares around the shape one-by-one (as if it is a picture frame), including the four extra squares in the four corners and thereby getting the wrong answer

❖ Counting a frame of squares just inside the shape, but along the perimeter, thereby missing some edges (the squares in the corners each have two edges along the perimeter)

❖ Counting the squares outside the shape, skipping corner squares, but undercounting the edges on concave corners (see Figures 5a and 5b)

❖ Using the measurements of each side and adding them (not making use of the fact that opposite sides are equal)

❖ Measuring one side, doubling it, then counting the adjacent side, doubling it, then adding together

❖ For non-square rectangles, adding length plus width and doubling the sum

❖ For the square tables, multiplying the length of one side times 4.

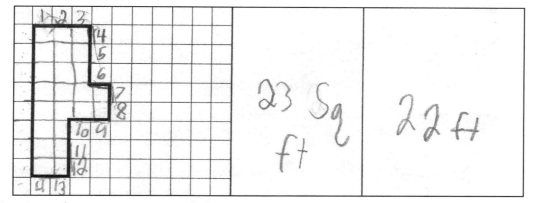

Figure 5a. A student counts around the perimeter, missing one line segment at each of the concave corners.

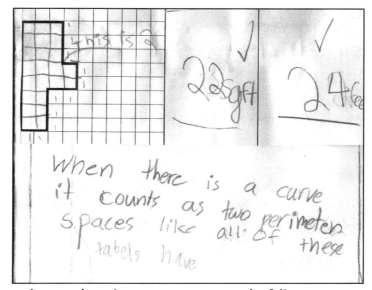

Figure 5b. Students understand perimeter as composed of line segments rather than boxes. "When there is a curve it counts as two perimeter spaces."

As you confer with students, encourage them to look for efficient ways to find both the area and perimeter. For those students who are counting squares instead of edges, stay grounded in the context. Remind them that the perimeter is about the length of the tape. Ask them where the tape will go, ensuring that they understand it is a strip that goes around the edges of the table. You might ask them if both sides of the corner tile count as length of tape. Or, if they have built a sort of picture frame around the table, ask about the 4 extra tiles in the corners. What part of the tape are those tiles touching?

Two of the tables in Appendix E are drawn against an edge (or "wall") with no tile markings to guide students. These tables serve as opportunities to challenge students who are counting the tiles outside each edge. There are no tiles past this edge, but it still has length. How long is it? Students will need to reason with the properties of rectangles to find out, perhaps discovering a need to use equivalent lengths and use a doubling strategy.

Regarding the perimeters, are any students wondering what happened to the original perimeters when tables are recombined? What about the exterior edges of the original tables that are now interior edges? Encourage students to notice relationships between the tables. For example, on Appendix E, table 5 has an area of 4 square feet and a perimeter of 8 feet. Table 3 has twice as much area, but the perimeter did not double: it is 12 feet. Let students grapple with this and encourage them to explain why the perimeter did not double, too.

Inside One Classroom: Conferring with Students at Work

Pamela and Roy are working on Table 1 found in Appendix E. To determine the perimeter they count each square (suggested by the grid lines) around the gray 3x3 rectangle, producing a measurement of 16.

Pamela: So that's 16. I counted these squares. They go around the table.

Becca (the teacher): It looks like you are using the grid lines as a tool?

Roy: Yep. We sort of thought of these as squares, and so we counted them.

Becca: What a good idea to use the squares! So where is the tape going? Where is the edge of the table?

Pamela: The tape goes around the table. That's why we used the squares. They go around the table, too.

Author's notes

Becca starts the conferral by listening intently first and noting the strategy the children are using. She asks for clarification to make sure she understands. This is part one of a conferral. Then she supports by celebrating what they have done so far: their strategy of making use of the grid lines as a measurement tool. This is part two of a conferral. Then she moves to part three— probing further and challenging to support development.

Becca: That is what I thought you said! And that is really an important noticing. Is the tape going on top of all the squares, or somewhere else? Is it the squares you want to count, or the edges of the squares?

Roy: That is the same number though, I think....oh, maybe not...

Pamela: Oh yeah! You are right, Roy. It's not the same. It's just the edge that matters! The tape is measured in feet, not square feet. These squares in the corners don't even touch the edge of the table. They are extras.

Roy: Oh yeah! So it isn't 16; it is only 12! We had extras.

The two students are now considering the difference in measurement. The squares can be helpful as a tool, but it is only the edges that matter. Perimeter is a linear distance. The edge of the square and the edge of the table can be thought of as lines, bordering both the square and the edge of the table. These can be units of linear measurement.

As students begin working on Appendix F, the combined tables, don't tell them that there is no need to measure area because the areas of the original tables are now just combined. Let them discover this. First, this is an opportunity for them to construct conservation of area. But, secondly, realizing that different shapes can cover the same area is a huge developmental leap for children. This idea requires an integration and synthesis of part/whole relations. It is in fact an important precursor to developing the ideas of composing and decomposing areas, which will be needed much later in development (in other grades) as they engage in constructing area formulas for polygons. It is also important for them to realize that shapes do not have to be congruent to have the same areas. These are big ideas about area for them to bring back to congress and defend on Day Six.

As students prepare their work on the large grid paper, remind them to record any interesting connections they noticed and to write convincing arguments, rather than just retelling "what they did" step by step.

Reflections on the Day

Today students were asked to measure area and perimeter of tables, both the original tables in the art room and the combined tables after Ms. Suarez joined certain tables. As area is becoming more comfortable for many students, and perimeter is beginning to get more attention in the unit, you probably saw a range of strategies used for perimeter and area and perhaps you heard lively conversation about the relationship between the two. The big ideas of area and perimeter, decomposing and recombining will be the subject of tomorrow's math congress.

DAY SIX

CONNECTING THE TABLES

Materials Needed

Students' work from Day Five

Large chart paper prepared with Venn diagram

Definitions of Polygon and Quadrilateral posted

Art Table Shapes (Appendix G, one per pair of children)

Today begins with a minilesson on the use of partial products. Students then add finishing touches to their posters and engage in a gallery walk and a math congress. In the congress, strategies for finding the area and perimeter of the separate and combined tables in the art room are discussed. At the end of the math congress, class inclusion will be revisited when students categorize both the original and combined art table shapes and discover that they are all polygons, but not all are quadrilaterals.

Day Six Outline

Minilesson: a string of related problems

❖ A string of related problems is used to support the use of the properties of multiplication: associative, commutative, and distributive. As students share, represent their strategies using the open array model.

Facilitating the Gallery Walk

❖ Conduct a gallery walk to allow students time to reflect and comment on each other's posters.

Facilitating the Math Congress

❖ Convene students at the meeting area to discuss a few important ideas on the landscape about area and perimeter.

Minilesson: All Polygons are not Quadrilaterals

❖ End today with a short minilesson using a Venn diagram. Have students decide which category the art tables go in: polygons, quadrilaterals, or both.

Minilesson: a string of related problems (10-15 minutes)

Today begins in the meeting area. This string of related multiplication problems continues the minilesson work from Day Three on the associative and distributive properties of multiplication. The string is designed with related problems to support students to move from counting squares to more efficient area strategies that make use of the properties of multiplication. Model student thinking using open arrays and call them the art room tables when you think it would be beneficial to ground students in the context of yesterday and today's investigation.

3 x 2	**Behind the Numbers**
3 x 3	These numbers were chosen, first and foremost, because they are related and will engender a discussion of the properties of operations. Secondly, they use the measurements of the art tables from yesterday's investigation. The first three sets of three problems represent two tables being "pushed together" resulting in the third rectangle, with one more challenging problem at the end of the string. Most students will have either memorized 3x2 or quickly think of 3x2 as three 2s and easily get 6. 3x3 is another art table measurement and shares one of the side lengths with 3x2. When modeling student thinking for 3x5, ask students if it works to "push together" the 3x2 and 3x3 rectangles to make a 3x5 rectangle. This is a good opportunity for pair talk and reflection as discussion will likely generate the use of partial products and the underlying big idea: the distributive property. 2x2 and 2x4 can be "pushed together" to make a 2x6. 4x5 and 3x4 are intentionally reversed so that students are challenged to make use of the commutative property: 3x4 can be rotated, resulting in 4x3, which can then be "pushed together" with the 4x5 to result in the 4x8 rectangle. The final problem, 4x13, will likely be a stretch for many students, but there are several problems in the string that can be combined to make a 4x13 rectangle. Invite several strategies, and model them on arrays as partial products.
3 x 5	
2 x 2	
2 x 4	
2 x 6	
4 x 5	
3 x 4	
4 x 8	
4 x 13	

Inside One Classroom: A Portion of the Minilesson

Becca (the teacher): This is so exciting with all of the relationships you are noticing! It's almost like the tables you've been working on! And now we are at the end of the string with just one last challenge. What can you do with this one? *(She writes 4 x 13.)* Turn to a partner and talk about this one. Not such an easy one. Can you find a way to make it easy?

(As the children talk, Becca moves around and listens to some of the conversations. After a few moments, she starts whole group discussion.) Did anyone have an interesting partner?

Author's notes

As Becca moves to the last problem in the string, note how she solicits several possible solutions. Thinking is at the heart of this work, not just one answer.

(The children are surprised by her question and had been prepared to share only their own ideas, so no one puts a hand up. Nonplussed, Becca continues.)

Well now that is a pity, not one interesting partner in this whole community of mathematicians? Well then, turn and talk again. Be an interesting partner.

(Now there is a real "math buzz" and after a minute Becca resumes whole group discussion.) Carl, I saw you and Claude using your hands like you were chopping something off. Start us off. What were you talking about?

Carl: Claude and I were saying that we could split the 13 into an 8 and a 5. So we just used the problems we did earlier, 4 x 5 and 4 x 8.

Becca: Oh, now that is interesting, isn't it! So can I write this to represent your thinking?
(She writes: 4 x 5 + 4 x 8 = 4 x 13 and draws the array.)

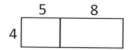

Is this what you mean? These two tables put together make a 4 x 13? Everybody, turn and talk with a partner again. Are they right?

Yolanda: Yes! And Claire and I found another way, too. We used 4 x 5 twice and then we used 3 x 4 and we turned it.

Becca: *(Writes 4 x 5 + 4 x 5 + 3 x 4 and draws the arrays.)* Wow. Let me make a picture of that. You turned the 3 x 4 into a 4 x 3? *(Becca draws the pieces under discussion using connected open arrays.)*

Becca: So this is also a 4 x 13, huh? Two great strategies! Does anyone else have a strategy to share?

Becca provides time for pair talk as a way to push reflection. By asking if anyone had a helpful partner, Becca is implicitly communicating that during pair talk each and every student should try to be an interesting and helpful partner. Talk must be "accountable talk" in a community of mathematicians at work.

Becca has succeeded in getting partial products up for discussion again. By using the open array as a representational tool and building a connection to the tabletop areas, Becca supports students to visualize how the parts are moved without changing the area.

Becca represents a second possibility and continues the discussion by asking if there are even more.

Facilitating the Gallery Walk

After the minilesson comes to an end, direct students to finish their posters from Day Five. As students work, make sure they have calculated both the area and the perimeter of the shapes. Once you have given students sufficient time for this, hand out sticky notes and reiterate gallery walk norms (see the Teacher Note for Day Three for suggestions). Begin the gallery walk, and encourage students to comment on enough posters so that every poster has some comments.

After the gallery walk, allow students a few minutes to read and discuss the feedback they received before gathering your class in the meeting area.

Facilitating the Math Congress

As you observe posters during the gallery walk, select a few that will develop the big ideas on the area and perimeter landscape. The purpose of this math congress is twofold since we are working today with both area and perimeter. For perimeter, choose posters that will help move your class toward more efficient ways of finding perimeter, such as adding, doubling, or even multiplying, in some cases, a side length by four. For area, look for posters that scaffold strategies, perhaps ending with a poster in which students added composite areas together to result in the total for the shape.

You may decide to have a group only explain their strategy for area or perimeter, as the groups won't necessarily have used efficient strategies for both. For instance, if one partnership had an efficient strategy for doubling opposite equal sides to calculate perimeter, but counted squares one by one to find area, you may want them to focus on explaining only their perimeter strategy. If any students are still struggling with extending the gridlines to show square tiles, be sure to choose a group to discuss this crucial big idea. If some students made errors while counting around the shapes to find perimeter, choose a poster that shows an organized approach to counting or one that clearly shows counting both exterior edges at the corners. Of course, if any group added or even multiplied, where possible, whole side lengths to find perimeter, that would be a good poster to put at the end of the congress.

Look to develop the big ideas that the combined tables are made up of the total areas of the smaller tables, but that the total perimeter is now the combined total of only the new side lengths. Compare the perimeters of the combined tables to the original tables and pose the question of what happened to the interior edges once tables are pushed together. All in all, the math congress today should move your students further along the area and perimeter landscape, introducing them to more efficient and accurate strategies for finding area and perimeter of larger rectangles and composite shapes. These new rectangle strategies will be particularly helpful in Day Seven's investigation.

Minilesson: Sorting Polygons and Quadrilaterals

Make sure to leave sufficient time at the end of math today to bring students' attention back to another big idea of this unit, shape classification. Are the original and combined art room tables quadrilaterals? Are they polygons? Are they both?

Post the Venn diagram you have prepared with overlapping circles for polygons and quadrilaterals. Nearby, post the definitions of a quadrilateral and a polygon. Because you will probably be short on time at the end, it will help if you have affixed some rolled tape or magnet clips to the shapes beforehand. Display the shapes where students can ponder their placement. After students have had some think time, ask for thumbs up to place the pre-cut shapes from Appendix G, which are similar to the art room original and composite tables, where they belong on the Venn diagram.

When students are done, they will be able to see that all of the original tables are in the both category—the intersection—and all of the combined tables are only in the polygon category. None of the shapes are only in the quadrilateral category. Ask students why this is. Hopefully they will have developed the idea of class inclusion: in this case, that all quadrilaterals are also polygons, but not all polygons are quadrilaterals. It will also bring students' attention to how many sides the combined tables actually have, as they explicitly have to count them for this activity. This will highlight the fact that if rectangles are joined but do not line up exactly, the resulting shape has more than four sides.

Teacher Note

Many teachers are familiar with the use of Venn diagrams as a graphic organizer in literacy instruction. Two overlapping circles might represent two people, for example, giving space to write the attributes of one character alone, of the other, and attributes the two share in the middle. We might use the tool similarly in mathematics, listing the attributes specific to one shape, to another, and attributes both shapes share. However, we can also flip the Venn diagram and use the circles to represent attributes or categories, while the space inside the circles is used for shapes or numbers that are members of each category. This is the same way we have used isolated circles in previous minilessons. With two circles representing categories,

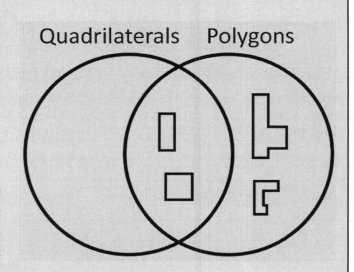

the overlapping section in the middle is filled with shapes that are members of both categories. Note that the intersection of the two circles is the only correct space to place these dual-member shapes. If a square were placed in the "quadrilaterals" category but not also in the "polygons" category, that would imply that a square is not a polygon when in fact it is. Attending to this important aspect of the diagram's structure will help students identify that there are no possible shapes that are quadrilaterals without also being polygons; an important noticing grounded in class inclusion.

Reflections on the Day

Students shared and reflected on their work finding the area and perimeter of slightly larger rectangles, and had their first experience finding the area and perimeter of irregular shapes. The minilesson at the beginning of class further developed partial products, or the distributive property of multiplication, while the minilesson at the end of the class gave students the opportunity to deepen their grasp of shape categories. The gallery walk allowed them to consider their classmates' various strategies for finding perimeter and area and the math congress provided a chance to have a rich discussion about area and perimeter, discovering that the area of each of the combined tables is the total of at least two of the original tables joined together and that in order to find perimeter, you have to add up the total of all of the exposed side lengths, not just add up the perimeters of the original tables. Tomorrow, students will build on their understandings of area and perimeter when the context moves outside. On the field, gridlines are replaced with measurements, further encouraging students to replace counting strategies with multiplicative ones.

DAY SEVEN

THE FIELD

Materials Needed

The Field (Appendix H, one per pair of children)

Large chart paper for student posters

Markers or colored pencils

A meter stick

Today students are pushed to consider the properties of rows and columns and the relationship of multiplication to area. Given a large field with no tiles or other gridlines, students must reason about the spatial relationships to determine the area and perimeter of the field.

Day Seven Outline

Minilesson: Doubling and Halving

❖ A string of problems supports the use of the associative and distributive properties of multiplication to make multiplication problems with larger numbers more accessible to students.

Developing the Context

❖ Introduce the diagram of the field and its two side measurements.

❖ Students may want more information than the diagram contains—challenge them to reason about what information they can determine for themselves using the properties of rectangles, area, and perimeter.

Supporting the Investigation

❖ Some students will enjoy the new challenge of the field, while others may feel overwhelmed. As you confer, support partnerships who are struggling to draw the field and find pieces they know, so that they begin to shift their thinking from additive (repeated addition or skip-counting) to multiplicative structuring (using pieces they know and building from there).

Minilesson: a string of related problems (10-15 minutes)

Gather students in the meeting area and remind them to give you a private "thumbs up" when they've had enough think time for each problem. Utilize group discussion and pair talk as necessary to ensure that students are reflecting on the connection between the problems. Today's string is designed to help students use the associative property, especially doubling and halving and multiplication by ten, to transform the larger area they will encounter in today's investigation to expressions with easier calculations. Model students' reasoning using open arrays, which can be partitioned and rearranged to show the relationship between problems and subtly emphasize the connection between multiplication and area.

The string:

6 x 5

12 x 5

6 x 10

3 x 20

100 x 2

50 x 4

25 x 8

Behind the Numbers

6x5 is a multiplication fact many students will have memorized. Others may skip-count by fives to find the product. 12x5 is harder, but some students will likely realize it is a double of the first problem. 6x10 is also double 6x5, and now doubling and halving may emerge for a discussion because the answers of the second and third problems are the same: 12x5 = 6x10. Halve and double again, and you have 3x20. 100x2 starts a new sequence of products. 50x4 may be doubled and halved to yield 100x2 again, or may be seen as 5x4x10. Finally, 25x8 is a challenge. Remind students to use the patterns that have been useful so far in this string. If students rely on skip counting or their knowledge of money, help them discuss why the answer turned out to be 200 yet again.

Developing the Context

Students should now be comfortable with the concepts of area and perimeter, having explored them in the context of floors and tables in two different classrooms. So far, gridlines have supported students who used counting and additive strategies to calculate the area. In the field, however, the numbers are larger and there are no gridlines. Students may use their knowledge to generate helper lines, but many will opt for more efficient multiplication strategies that don't require an explicit grid to calculate the desired values. Appendix H is designed to make drawing all of the gridlines difficult. This is purposeful to encourage students to make use of what they know to determine information they don't know. Using the picture in Appendix H, introduce the context to the students as follows:

There is a field behind the school for sports and other outdoor activities. Two of Mr. Forest's students measure and find that the side of the field closest to the school (running east/west) is 50 meters long. The side going back away from the school (running north/south) is 30 meters long. Two of Mr. Forest's students are discussing the area and perimeter of the field.

"That's it!" says Saadia. "It's 30 meters by 50 meters. Let's go back inside and find the area and perimeter."

"Are you sure we have enough information?" asks Aniyah.

"Yes!" responds Saadia.

Is she right? Here is a diagram of the field. (Show Appendix H.)

Divide the students into pairs and distribute Appendix H. As students begin to think about the context, this may be a good moment to remind them to pay attention to the units given in measurement contexts. A field is a lot bigger than a classroom! In this problem, the distance around the perimeter will be measured in meters and, since area is measured in square units, the field's area will be measured in square meters. You can use the meter stick and mark out a square meter on the floor to help students to visualize this new measurement unit.

Supporting the Investigation

Today's investigation may be a challenge for some of your students. There are no gridlines and no tiles to count. Many students may want to draw in gridlines. Encourage these groups to look for more efficient strategies. It would be hard to be accurate drawing 50 spaces, and it would also take a really long time! Can students imagine the field in rows and columns of square meters? Can they skip-count or make groups based on knowing the number of meters on a side? As they strategize to avoid counting by ones, groups will likely break the field into friendly partitions. Some may start with one column of 30 (in an open array style) or a row of 50. With these students, ask them to find pieces they do know. How many square meters in one column, or two? What about 10? Can they image 10 x 30? Or, they may be able to picture 50 square meters in a row. What about two rows, or ten?

Other students may split the field into five columns and three rows using a gridline every ten meters. There are now 15 big squares, but how big are those? This is a perfect moment to reinforce the big idea that square units are formed by multiplying the side units. Encourage them to do each column, using 10 times, as shown in Figure 6.

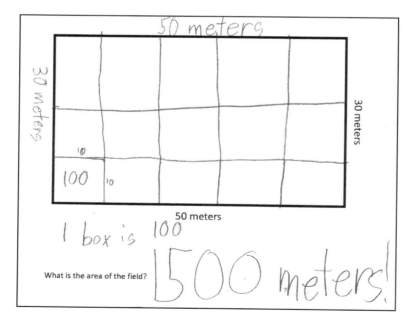

Figure 6

Still other students may be ready to begin with larger chunks right away, such as three 10x50 rectangles. Decomposing and recombining the field will strengthen students' facility with the distributive property of multiplication, as well as their understanding of the connection between multiplication and area.

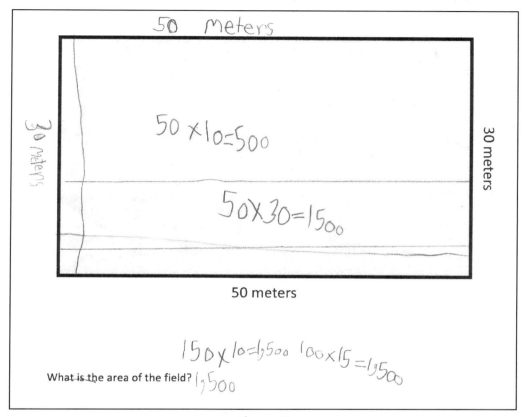

Figure 7

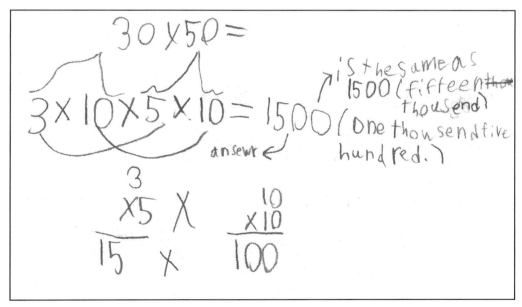

Figure 8

In Figure 8, the children have used the associative property but may not realize that they have produced 30 x 50 = 15 x 100, a specific case also of halving and doubling. When conferring with pairs like these a good question would be, "So are you saying that 30 x 50 = 15 x 100?" If the pair agrees the two expressions are equal you might also ask about halving and doubling since this was the discussion in the minilesson. You might write, 15 x 2 x 50, and ask if when multiplying we could always move factors around to make the work easier. Support them to generalize the big idea of the associative property.

In calculating the perimeter, one side is 50 meters long and another is 30 meters long. Can students use that information to figure out the other sides, given that the field is a rectangle? Remind them about what they know about rectangles. On the smaller tables and floors, each side of the rectangle had a partner side with the same measurement. If we imagine gridlines in the field, will this property of rectangles still hold true? Yes! And now the perimeter problem is easy to solve.

On the other hand, some groups may simply double the sum of the two known sides. Help them generalize this idea as a way to find the perimeter of all rectangles. How will they convince their peers of their formula? Celebrate their invention and make them feel like fabulous mathematicians!

As students work, keep an eye on the energy level of the class. If students are feeling productive, let them keep working! If many groups seem to be stuck, however, or they are working on tedious skip-counting strategies and making a lot of arithmetic errors, consider ending class with a mini gallery walk and brief discussion of strategies students noticed. Students may not be ready to present their work yet, but you can ask them to lay out what they have done so far and invite them to visit a few other groups' work spaces. Gather the group together and ask them to share noticings, such as "I noticed that Peter and Diego used big sections to split up the field," or "Sophia and Eli found the perimeter without even finding the missing sides. They just doubled what they knew. Would this always work with rectangles?" These ideas will provide avenues for further exploration and provide deeper opportunities for understanding during the full congress on Day Eight.

Inside One Classroom: Conferring with Students at Work	
Cole and Harrison are having trouble getting started. They are convinced they need more information to calculate the perimeter. **Cole:** How can we find the perimeter if we don't know all of the measurements? **Harrison:** I know. This *is* a hard one. I don't think it's possible. The girl in Mr. Forest's class in the story is wrong. **Becca (the teacher):** How's it going with this one? It looks like you are really puzzled! **Harrison:** Yep. It's hard!	 *Author's notes* *Becca moves around the room, noting the strategies being used. Several of her students are having a hard time getting started. She sits with a pair to help.*

Becca: It is! Of course that is also what makes it fun, right? A puzzle worth cracking!! A mystery! What a good feeling you will have when you solve it! What shape is the field? Did you talk about that?

Cole: It's a rectangle, right Harrison? (*Harrison nods in agreement.*)

Becca: Sometimes when mathematicians feel stuck they stop and ask themselves what they do know, and they write that down. Why don't you start like that? Write down that the field is a rectangle. What do you know about rectangles? Do you know anything about the lengths of the sides? You could write that down, too.

Cole: Rectangles have 4 sides...like a quadrilateral. I remember that from the minilesson.

Becca: Wow! That's an important piece! Do you know anything about the lengths of the sides? Is a trapezoid a rectangle? (*She draws a trapezoid.*)

Harrison: No, because that side is too long. (*He points to the bottom length.*)

Cole: Oh! I got it, Harrison. The other sides have to be the same! It's a rectangle!

Harrison: Oh yeah! Good thinking, partner! Now we can do it! We just add up 30 + 50 + 30 + 50... all the sides.

Becca: Wow. This is so exciting what you are doing. Do you mean that 30 + 50 is this part and the other part is also 30 + 50? This part is the same as that part? Could you just double the first part?

Harrison: I think so....

Cole: Yes...we could! That part is 80 meters, so this part is 80 meters. 160 meters! (*Both boys are now grinning with excitement.*)

Becca: Wow. What a contribution to the community this will be! Will this work for all rectangles? If we know the length and the width can we just double the amount? How will you convince everyone?

She starts the conferral by listening intently first and noting why the children seem stuck. Note how she states that challenging problems are the ones worth doing. She mentors by modeling what a mathematician might do when stuck. Go back to what you do know. The role of the teacher is not to just facilitate; it is to mentor.

Drawing the trapezoid provides a counter example for comparison.

Becca has now challenged the boys to generalize for all rectangles and to consider a proof. Notice how she makes them feel that they have a very important thing to bring to the community—something that will be an important contribution. Not only is Becca mentoring them as mathematicians, she is building a community.

Inside One Classroom: Conferring with Students at Work

Emily and Harper are working at drawing lots of tiny boxes inside the field, and Becca listens to their conversation for a moment before joining in.

Becca (the teacher): How's it going so far? It looks like you are starting with counting by 10s here.

Emily: Yeah. We knew a 10 would fit on the side here and we're making more.

Becca: Nice idea! Ten is a nice chunk of the side here, but it looks like it's going to take a lot of boxes going across! Do you know how many?

Emily: *(Starts to judge based on the space across and the box she's drawn.)* Well, I'm not sure yet.

Becca: I think they measured that for us in the story. Each of these tens you drew is 1 meter across and 10 down, right? And they go all the way to the end of the field?

Emily: Yeah. And if I'm counting by ones... it would be 50 across!

Becca: So instead of drawing each one, maybe I could just put dots after the ones you've drawn ("...") and know there are 50? That's much easier!

Emily: Definitely. So 50 tens is 500.

Rebecca: Wow! That was elegant! And what about the rest of the field? What do you think, Harper?

Harper: Well, there are 30 all together going down. So that's two more 10s... *(Rebecca nods.)* ...so three 500s!

Author's notes

Becca selects a group that is struggling with a cumbersome, additive strategy. She meets them where they are, with 10x1 boxes starting to fill the field, and helps them access their knowledge of grids with a simple reminder to use the measurements provided.

Rebecca encourages the students to use the open array as a model of the problem.

Rebecca widens the conversation to make sure that Emily's partner is engaged. He's been following the dialogue and is ready to extend the multiplicative strategy to encompass the entire field.

Reflections on the Day

Today students stepped out of their comfort zone with gridlines and worked to extend their understanding of area and perimeter strategies, utilizing the properties of rectangles and multiplication to find the dimensions of the field. Some students may already realize that the area of a rectangle is equal to its length times its width, while others are still piecing together smaller areas to create the whole measurement. Tomorrow during the full congress on this work, there will be an opportunity to support others to further examine the relationship of area and perimeter and to structure area multiplicatively employing the use of the associative, distributive, and commutative properties.

DAY EIGHT

THE FIELD CONTINUED

Materials Needed

Students' work from Day Seven

Large chart paper for student posters

Markers or colored pencils

Prepared definitions of parallelogram and rhombus on chart paper

Sorting Parallelograms and Rhombi
(Appendix I)

Today students will finish their posters from Day Seven and present their work in a math congress. Discussion will focus on general strategies for perimeter and area of rectangles and how the properties of multiplication can be useful. Math workshop ends with a minilesson on rhombi and parallelograms.

Day Eight Outline

Preparing for the Math Congress
❖ Students revise their work from Day Seven and prepare posters to share their strategies with the rest of the class.

Facilitating the Math Congress
❖ A quick discussion of perimeter will probably suffice to convince all the students that the opposite sides have the same length.
❖ Call on several groups who have calculated the area of the field using different strategies. Compare the diagrams of their strategies with the numeric expressions they represent, focusing on how many different equivalent expressions can represent 30x50. Ultimately, students will discuss the idea that the area of any rectangle can be found by multiplying the length times the width, and that the distributive and associative properties can be helpful to use in the calculations.

Minilesson: Parallelograms and Rhombi
❖ Students revisit the definition of a quadrilateral and learn the definition of a parallelogram and a rhombus.
❖ Students sort shapes into/out of parallelogram and rhombus groupings and then have a final discussion on class inclusion with polygons.

Preparing for the Math Congress

Some students may have found values for the area and perimeter of the field on Day Seven, while others may still be working. All students will need to explain their strategies on a poster to share with their classmates. Remind students that their poster should not explain everything they tried or thought, but rather be a convincing argument of the important ideas or strategies they want to put forth as true and justify.

As students begin to work on their posters, some groups may want to add in gridlines or other details they did not need to complete their computation. To some students, including more detail makes their work feel more complete or correct, but it may also take them back to more inefficient strategies like counting. Some have a tendency to turn it into an art project or a "visual display." Gently redirect these groups by reminding them that mathematicians find efficient solutions more elegant and that they didn't actually need the gridlines—that was one of the most exciting parts of their work, and they want to be sure to share that noticing with their classmates.

As you confer with students, note where they are on the landscape. Are they comfortable with the organization of space into rows and columns? Are they comfortable partitioning? Are they ready for a discussion justifying that the area of a rectangle is always length x width and that its perimeter can be found using 2 x (length + width)?

Facilitating the Math Congress

Today's math congress provides a rich opportunity to engage students in reflection on the properties of multiplication and how they can be modeled with open arrays. Students will have found the area of the field using a variety of friendly number groupings. These subdivided areas, or partial products, can be represented alongside each other by displaying several posters on the board at one time. Despite having different strategies, most groups will have arrived at the same answer.

As you select groups to present, one nice plan might be to begin with a group whose work will provide an opportunity to check that everyone understands that the two sets of opposite sides are equal lengths and, by extension, that each row or column will be the same length as all the others. With this organization of space established, call on a group to share how they determined perimeter. Support discussion on the use of the general formula: $P = 2 \times (L + W)$.

Next, move to a few posters that have used different subdivisions to calculate the area. If you have a group that was able to multiply 30x50 directly, consider having them go first to create a question in their classmates' minds. Does that shortcut strategy work? Then move to a partial product strategy to check it out and discuss how, for example, $30 \times 50 = (10 \times 50) + (10 \times 50) + (10 \times 50)$.

If a group has doubled and halved using $15 \times 100 = 30 \times 50$ you might consider using this strategy last. Focus discussion on verifying why it works. Have students show how the 30 x 50 array can be decomposed and rearranged into a 15 x 100 array, and write the equation: $15 \times 100 = 30 \times 50$. It is important to get students comfortable with equivalence representations like this instead of always just writing the answer after the equal sign. If appropriate, remind them of the last problem in the string during the minilesson on Day Seven.

Perhaps end the congress with this challenging question:

> Could we have predicted that 10x50+10x50+10x50 would have been equivalent to 3x10x5x10 or to 15x100? How?

This last question will really push students to examine the properties of multiplication.

Inside One Classroom: A Portion of the Congress

Becca (the teacher): Well, now that we've heard some strategies for the perimeter, let's discuss the area. I saw a lot of interesting strategies! Yuri and Fiona, why don't you share your work?

Fiona: Well, we got 1500. We cut it up by 10s and counted 15 boxes.

Yuri: Yeah. So we thought it was 150 because each box was 10, but then you showed us the 100-flat and we realized there were 100 meter squares in each of our boxes. So there are 1500 squares.

Becca: That's an important point, Yuri. Can anyone else explain for us why there are 100 squares in the boxes?

Valerie: It's 10 in each row, but there are 10 rows in each box. That's how I got 100 because it's 10 times 10.

Yuri: Yeah. It's times.

Becca: Sarah and August, this strategy makes me think about your poster. Could you bring it up to share?

August: Okay. We got 1500 too. Because 10x10=100 and 3x5=15.

Author's notes

This first partnership is still thinking quite additively. They drew gridlines on the rectangle and then counted the regions by ones. However, while preparing for the congress Becca noticed another group that might be able to connect this model with multiplicative reasoning. She has planned this conversation carefully!

Sarah: We got the same answer, but I don't think we did the same strategy. We didn't draw a picture. We just did 30x50.

Becca: That's an interesting question. Did Sarah and August use the same strategy as Yuri and Fiona? Or maybe a connected strategy? Or was it totally different?

Jason: They both did 10x10 and 15x100. Fiona and Yuri didn't do 3x5, but they could have instead of counting the boxes.

Valerie: Yeah. 3x5 is the big boxes and 10x10 is the square meters inside each box, and so 15x100 is all the square meters. I think Yuri and Fiona's picture matches Sarah and August's multiplication.

Emily: We did ten 50s first and then three 500s, but it's all the same problem! Ours was 3 times 10 times 50. You can do it in any order and it still works.

In fact, these groups were thinking quite differently. Because they decomposed the problem in similar ways, however, students are able to see how the properties of multiplication one group used are modeled in the open array of the first group.

With several different expressions on the board, even students who are reluctant to multiply will start to notice that, no matter how they skip-count, the same multiplication relationship keeps coming back: there are 30x50 square meters in the field.

Minilesson: Sorting Parallelograms and Rhombuses

After the congress wraps up, switch focus to a large piece of chart paper prepared with the definition of a parallelogram: "A parallelogram is a quadrilateral with two sets of parallel sides." You may need to remind students that parallel lines go in exactly the same direction and never cross each other. Draw a large circle below the parallelogram definition and display the shapes from the top half of Appendix I, asking students whether each shape belongs inside or outside the circle.

When students have placed these shapes, turn to a second (smaller) piece of paper with the definition of a rhombus: "A rhombus is a quadrilateral with two sets of parallel sides that are all equal in length." Displaying the shapes from the second part of Appendix I, ask which shapes belong in the rhombus group.

By this point, students have seen several examples of class inclusion. The square and rectangle included in the activity may help remind them that a square is also a rectangle, a useful analogue for the rhombus and parallelogram. Ask students:

❖ "What do you think the relationship is between a rhombus and a parallelogram?"
❖ "Could we put one circle overlapping or inside the other?"
❖ "Do you notice any other relationships?"

Students will have a number of relationships to debate. Not only is a rhombus a parallelogram, but so are all rectangles. A square is both a rhombus and a parallelogram. Though this was not explicit in your instructions, every shape in today's string was a quadrilateral—the entire papers with the parallelograms and rhombi could be placed inside a quadrilaterals group, which would then fit inside a polygons group. This is an exciting revelation for students, who will love playing with the relationships and building a chain of nested categories for the rhombus and parallelogram.

Reflections on the Day

As the unit begins to wrap up, students should be clear in their understanding that perimeter measures linear distance and area measures the covering without gaps of flat 2-dimensional space. They should be comfortable using partitioning strategies to facilitate the computation of area, and may even recognize that the area of a rectangle is always the length times the width. Hopefully, today's discussion provided an opportunity for all students to deepen their understanding of the connection between multiplication and area and to better understand how the properties of multiplication can be used to break down and recombine a multiplication problem.

DAY NINE

A CLASS CELEBRATION

Materials Needed

Appendix J (Appendix J, one copy per pair of children)

Today students arrange Mr. Forest's tables into a variety of new rectangles. Once again, they want to know the area and perimeter of each rectangle. By now, students should have a variety of efficient strategies to perform their computations and can also focus on the relationships between the measurements.

Day Nine Outline

Developing the Context
❖ Mr. Forest has decided to take his class out to the field to celebrate their hard area and perimeter work. The class is going to carry out all their tables and arrange them into one big rectangle that will be covered with brown paper.

Supporting the Investigation
❖ As students work to explore new rectangles, they have opportunities to try out or practice efficient strategies for finding the area and perimeter.

Facilitating the Math Congress
❖ Area and perimeter are related, but they are not directly dependent on each other. What measurements do determine the perimeter and area of a rectangle?

Developing the Context

Gather the students together in the meeting area for just one more investigation. Tell them a story with the following information:

> *Mr. Forest has finally made his decision and ordered twelve 2x4 tables for his classroom. To celebrate, he and his students carry the tables out to the field, where they plan to arrange the tables into one big rectangle for a class celebration. Putting the tables together, they discover four possible rectangles and make a chart to compare them (display Appendix K). One possible rectangle table will be 2 ft wide and 48 ft long. The others will be 4 ft by 24 ft, 6 ft by 16 ft, and 8 ft by 12 ft. How much brown paper will you need to cover the top of each table, and how much masking tape to go around the edges? Which do you think will be the best for the class party?*

Allow students to ponder this new task for a minute, and then remind students that over the course of your work with Mr. Forest's class you have discovered a number of efficient strategies for finding the area and perimeter of rectangles. As they work today, students should try to use elegant and efficient strategies so that they have time to explore as many rectangles as possible. Assign students partnerships and circulate to confer as they begin their work, recording their ideas on Appendix J.

Supporting the Investigation

The focus of today's task is exploring the connection between area and perimeter when the area of a rectangle is fixed by the context. (They should discover on their own that, with the same twelve tables acting as building blocks, no matter the arrangement the areas will always be the same, but the perimeter will increase as the dimensions diverge.)

Once students have found the area and perimeter of several rectangles, ask them what questions they have or patterns they may have noticed. Encourage them to investigate further to be able to explain and share these ideas.

Facilitating the Math Congress

When students have finished investigating, convene them at the meeting area for a final math congress. Likely, most students will not have had time to create a poster explaining their work; that's fine. Students have already presented and justified strategies for calculating area and perimeter on Day Eight. Today, the focus of the discussion will be on the relationship between area and perimeter.

On Days Three and Four, students investigated the relationship between two classrooms with the same perimeter but different areas. Today's work is the opposite, but supports the same conclusion: shapes can have the perimeter but different areas, or the same area but different perimeters. The linear dimensions of a rectangle can be used to find both its area and its perimeter.

Call on a few students to share one of the rectangles they found and how they calculated the area and perimeter for it. Record this information on a chart (similar to Appendix J) on the board or chart paper. It is likely that students will fairly quickly explain that the area always stays the same for every rectangle because the tables used are always the same. Still, ask students their strategies for double-checking the area, as this provides another opportunity to explore conservation of area and to notice (if they haven't already) that length x width produces the area.

Once your class chart has the area and perimeter of the four possible rectangles (2x48, 4x24, 6x16, and 8x12), discuss any patterns students noticed. Likely, students will mention that the long, skinny rectangles have the longest perimeter. This is a good moment to have students reflect on the relationship between the outer sides of each shape and the sides of the tables that are pushed together inside the larger tables.

Inside One Classroom: A Portion of the Congress

Becca (the teacher): Is Keith right? Is it possible that two shapes with the same area might not have the same perimeter?

Angela: Remember the art room! Mr. Forest and Ms. Suarez had the same perimeter, but it turned out that the art room was smaller. It had less area. *(Students nod in agreement.)*

Becca: Good point, Angela! So you're saying that having the same perimeter doesn't mean we have to have the same area. And what Keith suggested is the flip side of that?

Valerie: Well, it's always the same tables, so the area stays the same no matter what the shape of the rectangle is, because each time we are using all 12 tables. But sometimes you put the long edges on the inside and sometimes they're on the outside.

Becca: Turn to a partner and discuss what Valerie is saying. Do you agree with her? What does she mean by inside and outside? *(As her students engage in pair talk, Becca moves around and listens to several conversations. After a few minutes she starts whole group discussion again.)*

Author's notes

As the measurements for the four possible solutions go up on the chart, Keith proposes that two shapes having the same areas might have different perimeters. Becca uses this statement as the focus of discussion.

Valerie's point, that some of the perimeter gets lost when tables are placed side-by-side, is an important moment not to miss. Becca provides pair talk for reflection and small group discussion as a way to focus talk on the issue of why the perimeter is changing.

Becca: Max and Selena, tell the group what you have been discussing. **Max:** I get it! Valerie is right. Remember, the edges on the inside don't count for perimeter, so the more we put the tables touching each other, the less sides count. **Selena:** Right. We decided that the longer and thinner the rectangle became, the more perimeter it gained, because more of the edges of each table were on the outside.	*Providing pair talk at moments like this not only reengages children, it also provides important reflection time for learning.*

Reflections on the Day

Today students had another opportunity to explore the relationship between area and perimeter and to use the strategies they have been developing throughout the unit. They examined conservation of area and explored a group of rectangles where the area is fixed but the perimeter varies and began to draw conclusions about how the shape of a rectangle affects its perimeter, even though the area stays constant.

DAY TEN

SHORT MYSTERIES AND A DAY FOR REFLECTION

Materials Needed

Large butcher paper for the wall display (eight feet long or more depending on available space)

Students' work from throughout the unit

Drawing paper (a few sheets per child)

Scissors and tape

Markers

Today's math workshop begins with some short mysteries. Only a few measurements for some rectangles are known. Are these clues sufficient to figure out the missing side lengths, area, and/or perimeter?

The remainder of math workshop is then used for the development of a learning scroll—a wall display to represent the learning that has occurred over the course of this unit. To create this community scroll, students revisit the work they completed over the past nine days, retracing their thinking and charting the big ideas, strategies, and models that they generated and examined in their investigations. Questions that were raised but left unexplored are posted as possible future explorations for the mathematical community.

Day Ten Outline

Minilesson

❖ Explain that you know a few clues about some rectangles and you are wondering if the information is sufficient to determine what is unknown about each shape. Show one arrangement at a time and invite discussion.

Building the Learning Scroll

❖ Work with students to create a learning scroll to highlight the work they have done throughout the unit.

Minilesson: A string of related problems

Gather the students in the meeting area. Explain that in the minilesson today you are going to draw some rectangles and provide some clues and that you want the students to determine if there is sufficient information to figure out the other measurements. Draw a t-chart like the following on the side:

Length	Width	Perimeter	Area

As you progress through the minilesson, draw one shape at a time with the given dimensions and ask students to decide if they have enough information to figure out the others that are unknown. Elicit their ideas and justifications working toward group consensus and then fill in the t-chart.

The string:

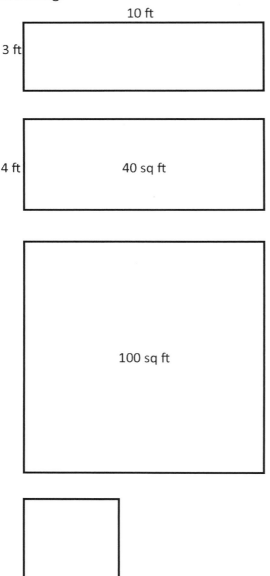

The perimeter is 16 ft.

Behind the Numbers

The first two shapes are non-square rectangles. The last two are squares. The first problem is a helper for the second. It provides students with an opportunity to use what they know and have been using over the last several days. The area can be figured by just multiplying: 3x10 = 30. Because it is a rectangle the other two sides can be inferred and the perimeter is then 2x(3+10). Division has not been introduced in this unit but the first problem may provide students with enough support to realize that 4x10 produces the area, and so now that they know the two dimensions they can also calculate the perimeter: 2x(4+10). As the string progresses, students will need to really think about the relationships of area and perimeter, all of the relationships they have been exploring as the unit progressed. The numbers used are easy to calculate to allow students to focus on the relationships and justifications, not the arithmetic. The third tectangles is a square (confirm this if children double-check with you), so all of the sides must be equal. 10x10 = 100, so the perimeter must be 4x10. The last problem may be a challenge, but the third problem may provide some support. The perimeter is 16 ft, and so each side must be 4 ft. The area is also 16, which may surprise students and provide an opportunity to remind them that the area is in square feet.

Building the Learning Scroll

As described in other units in this series, the primary purpose of a learning scroll is to give students an opportunity to reflect on their own thinking and then to consider how their ideas fit into and contribute to the mathematical learning of the entire classroom community. In this sense, it is a sociohistorical record of the learning over time, and a time for reflection. It is also an opportunity to emphasize the role that communication plays in mathematical life as students work to express their ideas, not just for their classmates, but also for the larger community.

Gather the students in the meeting area. Announce that you are going to create a learning scroll that will display all the work they have done over the past nine days as a record of their mathematical explorations and ideas. Invite students to reflect on their work over the course of the unit, thinking about what they have discovered and any questions they may still want to investigate. Their display will not only document this learning; it will also communicate the scope of their exploration and discovery to the rest of the school community.

Organize the students' work into piles for each investigation and begin with a list of the various questions students explored. Post the first question about the space on Mr. Forest's tabletops, and ask students to examine their work and think about what important ideas, strategies, and further questions came up in the discussion. As a classroom community, pick several pieces of student work that are representative of these big ideas, strategies, and questions. You may find that some questions have not yet been explored; these can be listed under a heading like "Our Questions for Future Exploration." Next, post the question about comparing the two classrooms, and continue the process with each of the investigations in the unit.

The main goal here is to create a living document that accurately reflects your students' experiences in this unit and that invites passersby to interact and post comments and ideas as well. The display should contain samples of students' work that exemplify their strategies, struggles, and questions. With the class, organize the final document in a way that clearly communicates students' development. Here are three big ideas to keep in mind as you organize this material:

❖ What were the questions the students explored? These should be clearly delineated.

❖ What did students learn? Find pieces of work that clearly represent the ideas developed by the classroom community.

❖ What questions were raised? Some of these questions have probably been answered; others may still need to be explored. This should be indicated on the learning scroll.

Reflections on the Unit

The mathematician Samuel Karlin once wrote, "The purpose of models is not to fit the data but to sharpen the questions." In this unit, the grid and array models helped students explore area, perimeter, and partitioning. As students developed understanding that a square in a grid is in both a row and a column simultaneously, they began to structure 2-D space in systematic ways. They were able to compare different shapes and discover that they sometimes have equivalent areas, or two shapes may have equal perimeters and different areas. The open array emerged as a tool to represent students' multiplication strategies such as partial products and eventually supported the generalization of area and perimeter formulas for rectangles.

Appendix A – Mr. Forest's Tables

How can four students share each of these tables? How much space will each student have?

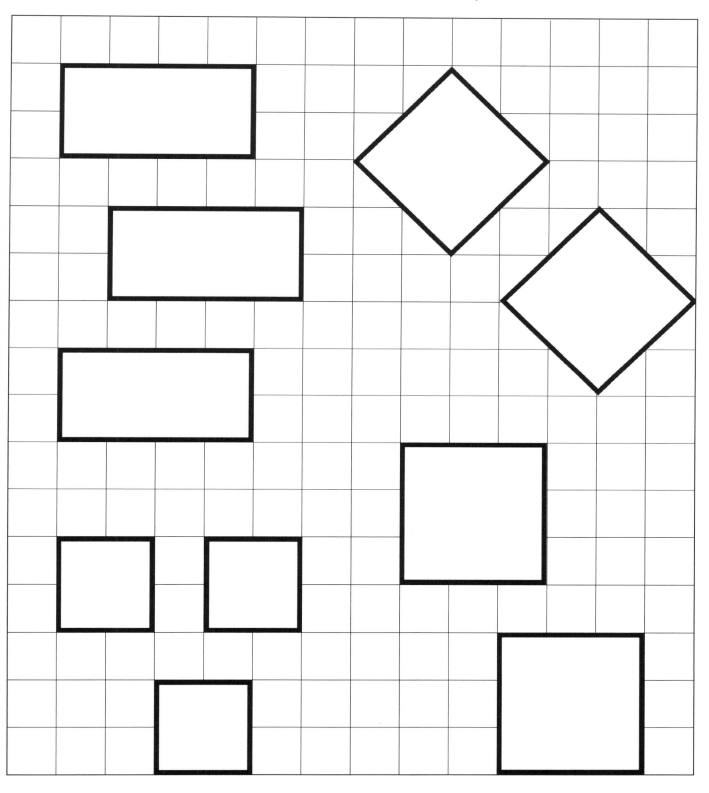

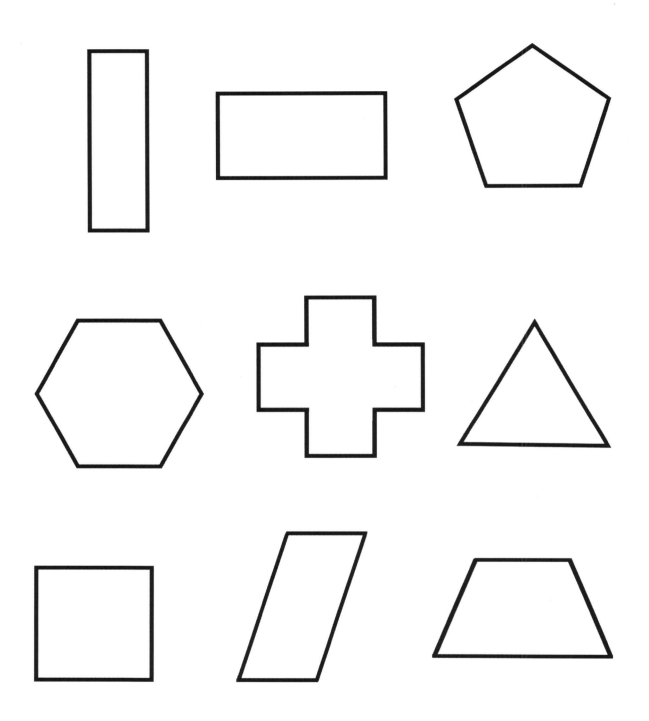

Mr. Forest's classroom is 20 feet long and 20 feet wide. What is the area of his classroom?

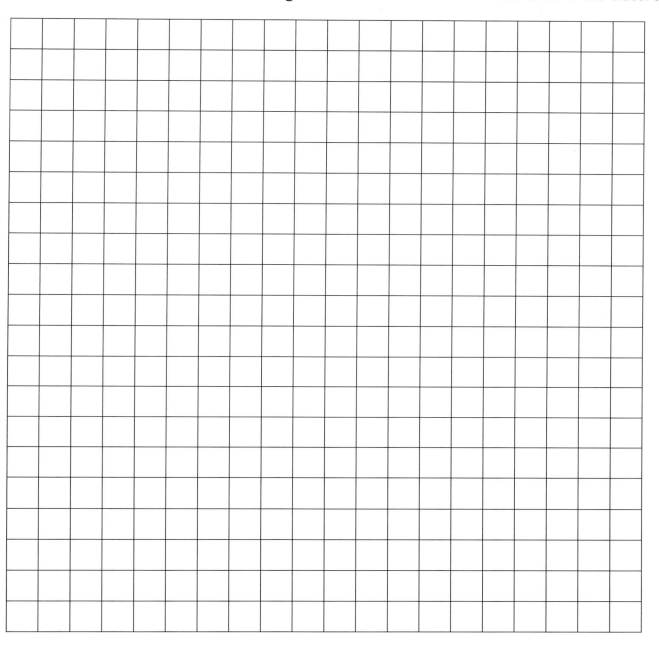

Ms. Suarez's classroom is 25 feet long and 15 feet wide. What is the area of her classroom?

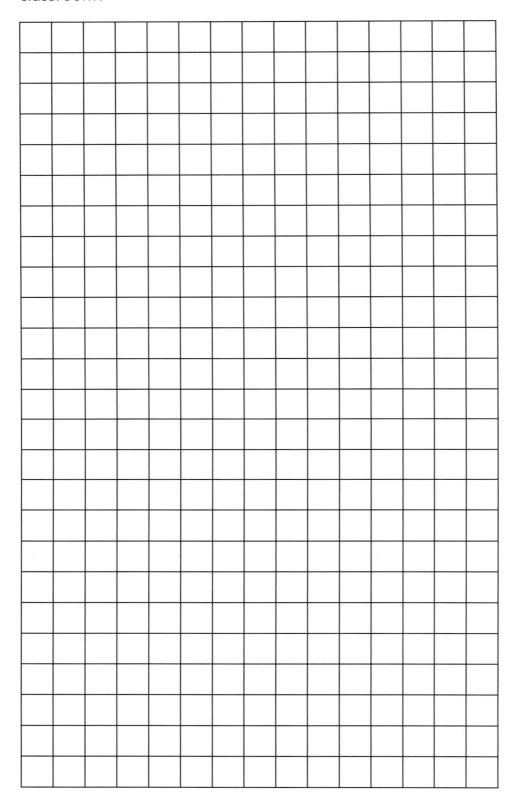

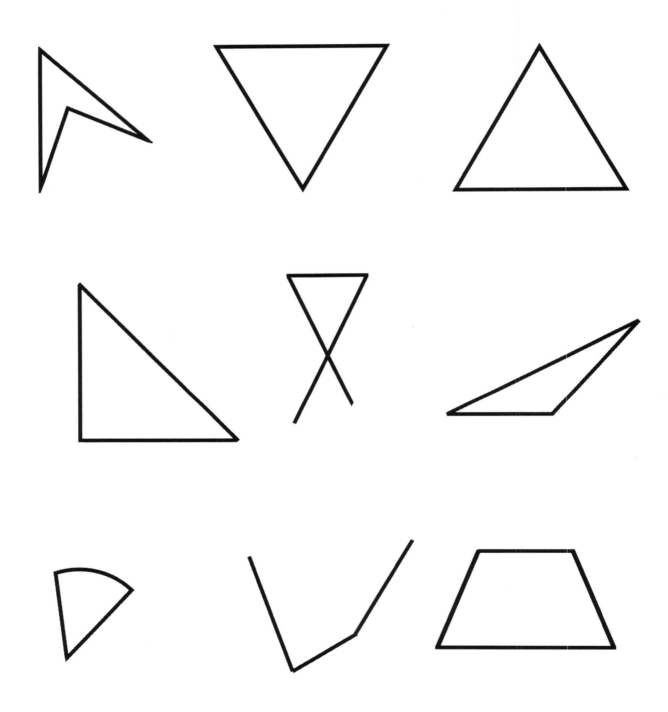

Table	Area of the table (space inside)	Perimeter of the table (distance around the edges)

Appendix F – Ms. Suarez's Combined Tables

Table	Area of the table (space inside)	Perimeter of table (distance around edges)

TABLETOPS, FLOORS, AND FIELDS: AREA, PERIMETER, AND PARTITIONING 80

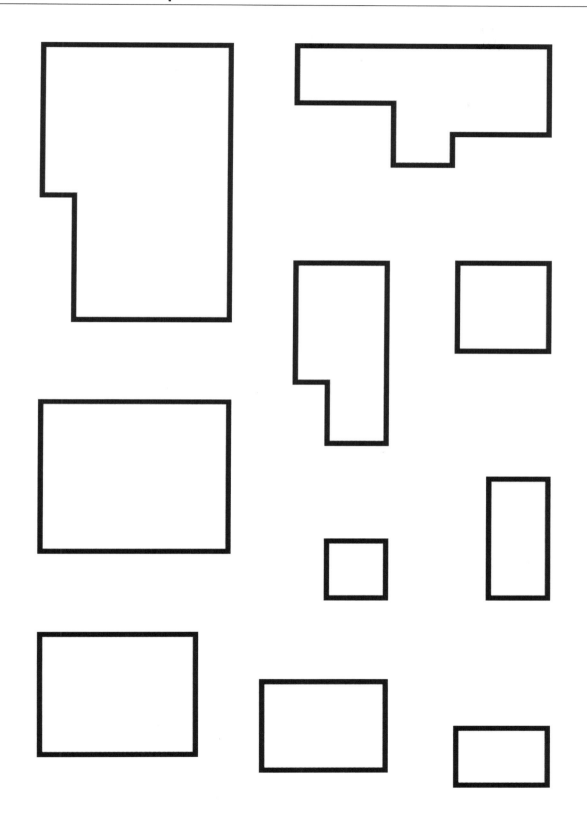

The field is 50 meters long and 30 meters wide.

30 meters

50 meters

What is the area of the field?

What is the perimeter of the field?

Are these shapes parallelograms?

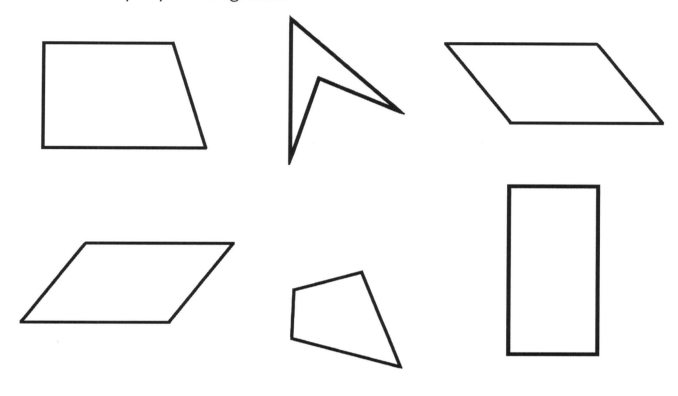

Are these shapes rhombi?

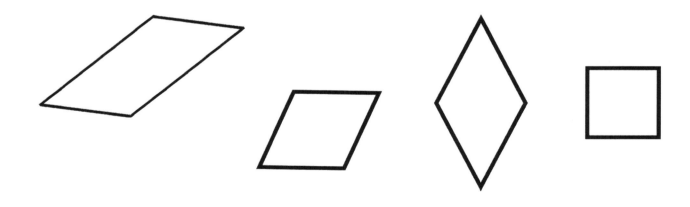

Appendix J – A Table for the Celebration

What are the areas and perimeters of the four large tables made from twelve 2x4 tables?

Dimension of the large table	Area of the table (brown paper needed)	Perimeter of the table (tape around the edges)
2 feet wide and 48 feet long		
4 feet wide and 24 feet long		
6 feet wide and 16 feet long		
8 feet wide and 12 feet long		

Printed in Great Britain
by Amazon

14455393R00050